THE RELIGIOUS TRADESMAN

vision harvest

good tools for home education, vocation, and your family

For other good and wholesome products, visit us online or request a free price list by mail or by phone. Every product we sell is reviewed and approved by a four-member product approval committee. Our selection criteria are very high. We offer a variety of products dealing with:

❧ Home Education
Homeschooling, distance learning, correspondence courses, apprenticeships, and skill-building products.

❧ Vocation
Trades, farming, home-based and family-run businesses, and man's calling by God (in particular his vocational calling).

❧ Your Family
Wholesome products for the family, including products for frugal and debt-free living, and books of high moral and inspirational content for individual or family reading.

Vision Harvest, Inc.
P.O. Box 680, Haymarket, VA 20168
703-754-0696 • info@vision-harvest.com

www.vision-harvest.com

Richard Steele's
THE RELIGIOUS
TRADESMAN

a modern English version by
RANDALL CALDWELL

First Printing: March 2005

First Edition
COPYRIGHT © 2005 BY VISION HARVEST, INC.
All rights reserved.

This book or parts thereof may not be reproduced in any form without written permission of the publisher. The only exception is brief quotations in reviews.

Vision Harvest, Inc.
P.O. Box 680
Haymarket, Virginia 20168
www.vision-harvest.com

ISBN: 0-9651332-2-2

All scripture quotations are from
the King James Version of the Bible.

Cover photo taken in the early 1900's. Used with permission of Vincent Crichton.

LAYOUT & DESIGN
BY VISION HARVEST

PRINTED & BOUND IN THE
UNITED STATES OF AMERICA

Table of Contents

	Preface	7
	To The Reader	9
	Introduction	11
1.	Of Business	13
2.	Of Choosing a Calling	23
3.	Of Prudence and Discretion	39
4.	Of Diligence	59
5.	Of Justice	69
6.	Of Truth	95
7.	Of Contentment	111
8.	Of Religion	129
9.	Of Leaving Our Callings	151
	Scripture Index	157

Preface

THIS BOOK IS AN EDITED VERSION OF A LONG ESSAY WRITTEN by Richard Steele in the early 1700s of the same title. The substance of the essay was itself taken from his earlier book entitled *The Tradesman's Calling*, which evidently had received little recognition, in part (according to its author), because of its lack of eloquent and scholarly language. In its original form, *The Religious Tradesman* is difficult going for today's readers. Its wisdom and practical advice are lost in its use of terms now archaic and its awkward sentence structures. Because of this, it has been given this fresh new look without removing the original meat.

To retain some of the book's original flavor, chapter titles, section headings and certain phrases often used by the author remained untouched, as was the note to the reader by Isaac Watts. In certain places, text was added to improve clarity. In other places, redundant or wordy material was removed to enhance readability. A brief appendix in the original edition was excluded, for it was reckoned irrelevant as well as grammatically problematic. An index of Scripture verses cited in the book has been added in its place.

While the goal was to convey the author's original intent,

there were a few cases where, for the sake of conscience, modifications were made. There are places in the original work, for instance, where the author may seem to support certain financial or business practices to which some may object, such as *business debt*. In these cases, a balance was sought that would retain the author's perspective as much as possible yet not violate the editor's conscience. Admittedly, this was likely achieved with varying degrees of success. Any resolution considered necessary is left to the discernment of the reader.

God has given men authority to name things, including book titles. While the meaning for the word *religious* was likely well understood in the culture in which Mr. Steele lived, it not so well-defined in the pluralistic society we live in today. Some now use the term *religious* to refer to those who have a form of faith in the Living God but not the substance of true faith, using the word *spiritual* instead to refer to those who have the latter. It was decided to define it as referring to those with true Christian faith, and ask the reader's charity wherever it is used in the book.

There were even concerns with the use of the word *tradesman*. It was clear that Mr. Steele used the word to identify a man whose business was the *trading of goods* and not a man who was *plying his trade* as in a craft or skilled trade. Realizing that its interpretation by many today would be the latter case, it was nevertheless decided to note the difference here and simply leave it as it was.

Finally, it is my hope that God receive the glory for anything that is good in this work and that those who may benefit from it will accordingly give credit to Whom credit is due.

Randall Caldwell
Virginia
March, 2005

To The Reader

THE REVEREND MR. RICHARD STEELE, A WORTHY MINISTER IN the last century, published a treatise entitled, *The Tradesman's Calling*; a book admirably fitted by its proper representation of the Tradesman's duties, and the close and warm enforcement of them upon the conscience, from the arguments of scripture and reason, to do excellent service (under the blessing of God) to the shop and to the world. This piece is now very little known; the chief reason of which may possibly be, that its noble matter lies under the disadvantage of an ancient name, and an ancient dress; to relieve which objection, and, if it please God, to do a kindness to the trading world, by setting before them their duty and interest, and thereby preventing those present and future miseries, which negligence, injustice, and irreligion, bring upon mankind; a person into whose hands it fell, from a strong persuasion of its admirable tendency to these ends, determined, after several alterations had been made, to send it abroad afresh into the world.

As it is a pleasure to meet with any opportunity to assist the cause of religion and virtue, and being well satisfied that the following sheets contain a rich treasure of wholesome instruction, such as every tradesman should write upon his heart, and practice in his shop and family, with the greatest readiness I lend my name to the piece; and heartily wish it could borrow much greater advantages, as to its perusal and usefulness, than I am capable of giving it by my recommendation.

As the age in which we live is much degenerated from the virtue and piety of our forefathers, I should be heartily glad if I might see the salvation of God, in a general repentance and reformation: And should this begin in the shop and the exchange, how wide and amazing would be its influence? No more would our eyes be witnesses of the base practices of overreaching, and various other iniquities; nor would our ears be so often shocked with the tremendous bankruptcy and ruin, brought by idleness, luxury and vice, not only upon single persons, but whole families left destitute and wretched forever after.

That the following pages may be blest to these purposes, is the desire and prayer of the Reader's hearty well-wisher and Humble servant,

Isaac Watts
Newington, England
January 24, 1747

Introduction

SINCE TRADE AND COMMERCE EMPLOY SO MANY PEOPLE IN the world today, any attempt to characterize all those who are happily and successfully engaged in it might appear to be a very difficult task. However, I think the difficulty can be reduced if we consider the moral and practical issues related to business. When it comes to fulfilling our common callings, we need to pay more attention to them than what is typically given. This book seeks to help out in this area. There is a very well-received book on the topics covered here, called the *Complete English Tradesman*, which I believe should be in the hands of all who are interested in the topic, although it considers the topic from a different perspective.

Instead of dwelling on speculative and controversial religious issues, here we will seek to consider various aspects of the calling of tradesmen, particularly with regard to a variety of other difficult issues. The tradesman must deal with the problem of the depraved nature of mankind as well as certain worldly temptations not found in other lines of work. Although the many aspects of the work of the tradesman are too numerous to be addressed here, I believe that the principles and rules presented in this book, when faithfully applied, will prove beneficial. Still,

THE RELIGIOUS TRADESMAN

given this, I believe that a healthy fear of God and a sincere love toward our neighbors will prove more helpful when certain difficult questions arise than what any book can reveal.

Let me ask readers to seriously consider the suggestions given in this book, and if you find they're consistent with reason and the laws of God, that you not fail to put them into practice. Surely, no one can be so absurd as to think it sufficient for them to appear religious on the Lord's Day, or to be serious in quiet prayer time, and then ignore matters of conscience at all other times. After all, such religious duties are intended to produce and maintain the principles of wisdom and justice, virtue and goodness, which are never to be neglected. Further, the Creator and Proprietor of the universe requires our constant obedience, as well as our devout worship and adoration.

I should mention that the substance of the material presented here is taken from a book entitled, *The Tradesman's Calling*, which although it has remained obscure, is thought by many to deserve greater attention. The publisher of the book might have had it revised or written by someone else, but he believes it may yet be useful, as one writer has observed, "Truth influences the mind of man more by its own authority, evidence and excellency, than by any ornaments of wit and eloquence in which it may be dressed." Such ornaments are not necessary in this case, because the subjects are written for the purpose of practical application. If God blesses the work so as to benefit the reader, the publisher will be fully rewarded for his work, whereas a thousand praises for its elegant composition, without such benefits, would be less satisfying. Several passages of Scripture have been added at the conclusion of each chapter, believing that God will always honor His own word.

Richard Steele

CHAPTER ONE

Of Business

*Man goeth forth unto his work and
to his labour until the evening.*
PSALM 104:23

THE HIGHEST PURPOSE OF MAN IS TO KNOW, LOVE, AND glorify God his Creator, Redeemer and Benefactor. However, since we've been designed to be mutually dependent on each other for our needs here on earth, by God's providence, both reason and religion require us to be employed in ways that benefit one another. Indeed, much of the beauty and excellence of the Christian life consists of this mutual dependency and benefit, using principles of wisdom, goodness, justice and integrity toward one another.

Both our real and imaginary desires have created great diversity in our occupations. Some are employed in the health field, while others work in the field of transportation. Some work in the area of education. Still others are employed in a vast variety of jobs that contribute to the conveniences and delights of mankind.

When we study the occupations of men we should do so by first reflecting on the wisdom and goodness of God. Some of us are endowed with extensive knowledge, others with vigor and strength. God gives to some great discernment while He gives others different gifts. Some are involved with travel abroad while others work in manufacturing at home. Everyone is called to serve the public good in some way.

It is God's will that we all find work corresponding to our vocational calling. God guides men according to such callings, which are both acceptable to themselves and useful to the community. Some find their labor to be tolerable and easy, while the work of others appears filled with hardship. Then there are the wealthy who should remember that their comforts greatly depend on the work of those who are poorer, and to treat them with tenderness and reward them liberally. In this way, "...the eye cannot say unto the hand, I have no need of you: nor again the head to the feet, I have no need of thee." (1 Corinthians 12:21).

That everyone who is capable of working should be employed in some way is a truth so evident that little needs to be said to support it. Indeed, no one has been created to always be idle or to be merely busy now and then as humor or fancy inclines him. We should be occupied with the business to which we are called, not busy concerning ourselves with the business of others. The wise Governor of the universe has called everyone to a certain occupation, and will rebuke rather than reward those who are busy with other activity.

REASONS FOR BEING OCCUPIED

Because excuses for both prideful and lazy behavior are plentiful, let me make several observations why we need to be occupied with useful activity.

1. *Most of us are not independently wealthy.* So it is both natural and reasonable that each of us have some form of work. It is also unreasonable for us to be dependent on others when there is no mutual benefit. To expect what we need for life will somehow fall from the clouds without our work is absurd, al-

though there are some who act that way by not being involved in some appropriate business for their own support. Regardless of our circumstances, the God of nature, who does nothing in vain and has given us certain abilities, has revealed to us that it is our duty to use our abilities in a rational and useful manner. Indeed, man is so naturally inclined to work that, if the law required him to be idle, many would willingly pay the fine for the liberty to work.

2. *God commands us to work.* Before the Fall, God chose a calling for Adam, "And the LORD God took the man, and put him into the garden of Eden to dress it and to keep it." (Genesis 2:15). Someone has observed that, "If a noble birth, as one observes, a great estate, a small family, and a mind fitted for contemplation, would excuse man from labor, none had so fair a plea for it as he." God has commanded of Adam's posterity, "Six days shalt thou labour, and do all thy work" (Exodus 20:9). This tells us that, over the seasons of our lives, we are to be actively involved with some form of employment. Scripture says, "Now them that are such we command and exhort by our Lord Jesus Christ, that with quietness they work, and eat their own bread." (2 Thessalonians 3:12). Christ Himself has provided us with an example through his work in the carpenter's trade. If so divine a Person stooped to such a laborious calling to teach us humility, diligence and industry, shall those who call Him "Lord" refuse to imitate Him by not working? It isn't that we should all be employed as carpenters, of course, but that we fill our time with appropriate and reasonable activities.

3. *Justice to our families and the public require that we not be idle.* Parents are naturally inclined to care for their children, doing that which promotes their well-being and happiness. However, laziness interferes with a family's blessings of happiness. Scripture tells us, "But if any provide not for his own, and specially for those of his own house, he hath denied the faith, and is worse than an infidel." (1 Timothy 5:8). How unnatural it is when children are deprived of the basic necessities of life because of a parent's laziness? How can we rise up and call them blessed who, because of this, make their children heirs to nothing but poverty and distress?

Neither should we overlook our public responsibilities. Everyone should be employed in ways that benefit the public good. Many of us will work to provide each other with conveniences and the necessities of life. Others who, by choice, do not add to the public welfare may risk losing certain public protections.

Given a conviction that idleness harms the morals of men, the ancient Greeks and Romans appointed rulers who would punish those who spent their time in sloth. It was the custom of the Jews to involve their children in some manual labor, regardless of their economic or educational status. For example, we find the Apostle Paul, who was educated under highly-regarded rabbis, working as a tentmaker. This custom has continued in other nations to this day.

4. *Our own safety and comfort greatly depend upon our not being lazy.* Like a bird in flight, those who remain busy don't usually fall into one of the many snares to which the lazy are exposed. Sometimes we find people who are unemployed for long periods of time, who are not doing what they should be doing. Such people become open to temptations. The wickedness of Sodom was the result of much idleness. Remember how David's sinful indulgences seem to have been proceeded by such periods? Honest work serves to minimize the pride, lust and sensuality that's so often produced by laziness. Sometimes, staying busy is better at restraining evil than the lawfulness of a particular activity. And many are those whose lives have been cut short or have suffered from diseases brought on by laziness, such as dropsy, consumption, melancholy, and the like. It is obvious that our use of the good things in life is greatly impacted by whether or not we stay busy.

No Excuse For A Life of Idleness

A slothful life is wrong, whatever excuses may be made for it. It is not right for those who are affluent to think themselves excused from staying busy. It would contradict God's revelation that much is expected from those to whom much is given. When this contradiction occurs, it often reveals ignorance in how one uses and appreciates their gifts. Such gifts can be particularly valuable in service to God, but are perverted when they're used to defend laziness. Even if someone is in a financial condition where they don't need to work for income, all benefit from his staying occupied, because idleness leads to many vices. When we don't keep our minds exercised, they can soon become corrupt. However, when we spend our lives in cheerful service to God and usefulness to mankind, we'll be pleased when we reflect back on our lives later on.

There are some who plead their idleness is merely part of their devotional life, but I fear that this is seldom the case, even among those who are affluent. However, it is especially vain when this excuse is given by those whose circumstances in life require them to be employed in order to support themselves and their family. I think it is grossly absurd for anyone to think themselves excused from their social responsibilities in life because of all of the attention they give to the external duties of religious worship. Here, I'm thinking of those who live as though they were all soul and had no body in this world, and who permit their families and business to languish because of their absence while they're indulging in zealous but mistaken piety.

Nor is it sufficient for someone to excuse himself because of his previous business failures. Because of his disappointment, let him exert greater diligence and prudence in his work, rather than use it as an excuse for laziness and despair. Some businesses succeed where others fail. When they fail instead of being discouraged, let the businessman be diligent to seek the cause of his lack of success and then work to correct it, regardless of whether the failures were the result of carelessness, laziness, lack of skill, lack of confidence, or corruption. Then, having done this, let him become involved in business again, using greater caution, with steady progress and diligence, and with a humble dependence on God, the Giver of wisdom and the Fountain of happiness.

If the problem is one of inability, be sure it's real and not imaginary. God gives everyone the ability to reason, and there usually exists some avenue for employment. In addition, we know that persistence conquers many difficulties that would otherwise go unresolved. Indeed, if we become completely disabled by such difficulties, God Himself will release us from that labor. This requires that we be patient and submit to His will. Unfortunately, there are those who seek to enjoy everything they can in life without working for it. It is their unwillingness to work, not their inability to work, which is the true cause of their life of idleness.

RESPONSIBILITIES OF PARENTS

Parents should seek to educate their children for a life of work and usefulness. For those who are rich, any wealth given them without requiring some work on their part will only serve to fuel their lusts, and help make certain their eternal ruin. In such cases of idleness, it is next to impossible to enjoy certain things of the world without becoming over-indulgent. On the other hand, if you're poor, you can similarly and permanently injure your children by allowing them to indulge themselves in idleness. Ultimately, this will lead them to shame and misery, and violate the trust that God has committed to you as a parent. It would be better for you to exhort them to an honest calling, where they might be happy in themselves, useful in the world, and respected by others.

Encourage the young to seek after useful knowledge, so they might find employment that benefits both their community and mankind in general. Although wisdom and knowledge can be difficult to obtain, and a life of ease can be a real temptation at the time, later on in life the fruit of hard work will be an abundant reward for one's labor and self-denial. We all have needs. But wisdom and knowledge are a blessing of heaven that come through hard work.

MATTERS OF RELIGION

How foolish it is when people neglect religion and the end of life, that is, in that which is so closely connected with the safety and happiness of our immortal souls. If hard work is so important to the common things in life, how much more important is it here. Our souls should be increasingly adorned with the image of God through a sincere faith in Jesus Christ and humble repentance before God. In this world, we're being prepared for final and everlasting glory. To this end we should be eagerly looking forward with full assurance of hope. This more than compensates for our greatest difficulties in life. Even children seem capable of realizing this, including people with sluggish minds and those who have no prospect of earthly honor or wealth in this world.

How preposterous it is when one overlooks matters of religion. Not only does this occur among those who are ignorant, indolent or slow, but also by the prudent and shrewd, by hardworking businessmen. There are those who rise early and go to bed late, who benefit from their labor for a little while, for temporary gain, but who are unable to find any time to think of God and their souls. They do this although they know by reason, conscience and the Word of God that such neglect is destructive to eternal happiness.

O, you, who work so hard! Are the brief and passing pleasures and honors of this life worth so much to you? Is it not important to you that, when these things fail, you may not have an eternal place of rest? Consider your ways and be wise. O, may God teach us all to distinguish that which is important and, by His grace, make us wise and happy forever!

SCRIPTURE REFERENCES FOR CHAPTER 1

"And she again bare his brother Abel. And Abel was a keeper of sheep, but Cain was a tiller of the ground." (Genesis 4:2).

"The sun ariseth, they gather themselves together, and lay them down in their dens. Man goeth forth unto his work and to his labour until the evening." (Psalm 104:22-23).

"The slothful man roasteth not that which he took in hunting: but the substance of a diligent man is precious." (Proverbs 12:27).

"In all labour there is profit: but the talk of the lips tendeth only to penury." (Proverbs 14:23).

"He that loveth pleasure shall be a poor man: he that loveth wine and oil shall not be rich." (Proverbs 21:17).

"By much slothfulness the building decayeth; and through idleness of the hands the house droppeth through." (Ecclesiastes 10:18).

"Who can find a virtuous woman? for her price is far above rubies. She seeketh wool, and flax, and worketh willingly with her hands.   She riseth also while it is yet night, and giveth meat to her household, and a portion to her maidens. She layeth her hands to the spindle, and her hands hold the distaff. She looketh well to the ways of her household, and eateth not the bread of idleness." (Proverbs 31:10,13,15,19,27).

"Behold, this was the iniquity of thy sister Sodom, pride, fulness of bread, and abundance of idleness was in her and in her daughters, neither did she strengthen the hand of the poor and needy." (Ezekiel 16:49).

"Now there was at Joppa a certain disciple named Tabitha, which by interpretation is called Dorcas: this woman was full of good works and almsdeeds which she did. Then Peter arose and went with them. When he was come, they brought him into the upper chamber: and all the widows stood by him weeping, and shewing the coats and garments which Dorcas made, while she was with them." (Acts 9:36,39).

"Yea, ye yourselves know, that these hands have ministered unto my necessities, and to them that were with me. I have shewed you all things, how that so labouring ye ought to support the weak, and to remember the words of the Lord Jesus, how he said, It is more blessed to give than to receive." (Acts 20:34-35).

"And withal they learn to be idle, wandering about from house to house; and not only idle, but tattlers also and busybodies, speaking things which they ought not." (1 Timothy 5:13).

"And let our's also learn to maintain good works for necessary uses, that they be not unfruitful." (Titus 3:14).

CHAPTER TWO

Of Choosing a Calling

*I would seek unto God, and unto
God would I commit my cause.*
JOB 5:8

NOW THAT WE'VE CONSIDERED CERTAIN RESPONSIBILITIES and benefits related to a life of business, we need to look at the matter of choosing a business. To some, this may seem so important as to impact not only this life but their next as well. And, speaking of choices, when we're young, our guardians or parents help make them. This doesn't mean that parents should ignore the natural gifts and interests of the child, however. There are several things that need to be considered when choosing an appropriate calling.

LAWFULNESS OF CALLING BEFORE GOD

Both the child and the guardians or parents must agree to choose a calling that is lawful before God. To commit a sinful act is bad enough. But to make a habit of it, by spending our lives in disobedience to God through their employment, is something that anyone with even a modicum of virtue remaining in them should abhor. Otherwise, they face the continual curse of God. When the prospect of material gain clouds the eyes of men and causes them to blindly follow a particular path, we often find that God's blessing is not upon them. We find their hopes and aims obstructed, and their vain attempts for wealth thwarted. This shouldn't surprise us. After all, God doesn't forget nor relinquish the right to punish behavior He disapproves of in this world. It is clear, although regrettable, that men today take great liberties with their consciences, and don't take their faith seriously, as if those things were limited to a few outward acts of piety, without having anything to do with their regular conduct.

It may be difficult to completely describe to a child those callings that are not lawful before God. Nevertheless, we need to acknowledge those callings that are evil, that tend to decrease the reverence and duty we owe to Almighty God, that obstruct the general good of mankind, or that tempt us or others to sin. We can reasonably ask God's blessings and expect His favor and acceptance only for lawful callings. Indeed, this is the best rule we can follow whenever we're making difficult choices.

SUITABILITY TO THE INDIVIDUAL

The choice of employment or calling must be suitable or fitting to the individual. The lives of people have been ruined and the public harmed when people choose their employment rashly or neglect important matters related to it. People become uneasy and discontented when they are employed with work that is beneath their abilities and talents. On the other hand, those who are employed with work beyond their abilities, after weak or unsuccessful effort, become discouraged. And, in this latter case, if they are placed in certain high-level positions, their weaknesses can become more obvious, and bring them to shame and rebuke.

One needs to consider both one's physical and mental abilities. Those with relatively little ability at remembering, decision-making, or self-control should obviously not be directed toward professions requiring ingenuity. Although some with limited abilities in these areas have been successful at such work, this doesn't justify our advising them to make that their choice. While

OF CHOOSING A CALLING

the Almighty God may do what He will, we must do that which is consistent with our design, including the gender and gifts given us by our Creator. Thus, a calling that requires much ingenuity should be filled by a man with much ingenuity.

On the other hand, it would be sad to confine a gifted person to employment that does not utilize his gifts. This would be like thrusting those to the oar who would be better at the helm. By giving certain people special abilities, God implicitly calls them to employment suitable to their abilities and consistent with their circumstances. God's method of calling men is not verbal but one that is expressed by how He bestows gifts to them. Similarly, our employment should be consistent with our physical abilities. Someone with a strong and healthy body accompanied by less mental ability is better suited for a more labor-intensive calling. Those who have less physical strength should be considered for less physically demanding employment.

We should also consider one's education and circumstances. For example, a liberal arts education should correspond with a calling suitable to such an education, all things being considered. A simpler education suits employment with simpler tasks. However, for someone to be content with such simpler tasks yet have much education and ingenuity would require unusual wisdom and humility.

The circumstances of people should also be considered in the choice of their calling. For example, it would seem absurd for those who expect to be employed in a high-level position to be placed into a low-level position instead. However, I think people more frequently err in the other direction. Because of their vanity and pride, people choose employment that is above their abilities, hopeful of some chance events that seldom come to pass. Because of this, they enter into business on a false foundation, which usually leads to significant disappointment, even ruin. Similarly, some, because of a lack of sufficient start-up capital, find themselves stuck in a state of financial dependency on others.

STEPS ON MAKING THE BEST CHOICE

To help make the best choice regarding one's calling consider the following:

1. *Give it the attention it deserves.* It's wrong to focus on such an important matter without giving it serious thought and reason. Yet, too often, it appears to be the frivolous things that guide people who are making this important decision. People often rush the issue of their employment, anticipating a life of ease or honor, pleasure or gain, only to discover that their expectations were unreasonable or excessive. Disappointed with their choice, they become restless and weary.

First, determine whether the calling you're considering is lawful before God and suitable for you. With sincerity, decide if you truly have the ability, time and resources necessary to learning what you will need to know. Ask yourself if you have the strength and patience to bear the type of burdens associated with what you want to do. If you do not, like the foolish builder, after you've laid the foundation, you'll not be able to finish, and expose yourself to sorrow and shame. If you're better suited to other callings, its wise and right to choose the one that best serves God and the community.

2. *Consult with faithful, discerning people, especially those with the same calling.* They're the best judges of their profession, since they know a great deal about its advantages and disadvantages, and the necessary qualifications. Therefore, give much weight to their advice, given their sound and faithful judgment. If you're advising someone else, convince them to ask the advice

OF CHOOSING A CALLING

of those with experience and honesty, and to use that advice when making decisions. Then, should they not be successful, they may be comforted by the fact that at least their problems were not the result of being rash. Later on, they'll be more likely to find others willing to help them, knowing they are not the type of man who makes hasty decisions.

3. Choose a calling that is not harmful to the soul. There are certain callings that are in themselves lawful and sufficiently profitable but, in the manner they exist today, would never be considered by anyone who cares for the immortal souls of them or their children. This is so because the temptations that come with certain occupations are so great that it is next to impossible to not be affected by the vice and immorality associated with them.

Similarly, there are certain places which might be preferred for business purposes yet, because of general neglect and evil influences in the area, have become as destructive as the type of work itself. Parents should give much attention to these matters. They should not expose the immortal souls of their children to such apparent hazards in anticipation of possible monetary gain, "For what is a man profited, if he shall gain the whole world, and lose his own soul? or what shall a man give in exchange for his soul?" (Matthew 16:26). Let the children spend time in places where God is reverently worshipped and their day spent dwelling on spiritual matters, where the weak and impulsive nature of their children is properly restrained, and where they will be taught how to live from an eternal perspective. Allow me to say that, if their lives and manners are not reasonably regulated by reason and religion, they'll be unable to find the type of happiness in this world that lasts.

4. Let God's providence be acknowledged by sincerely seeking His direction and assistance. God determines the limits and places in which we live, that by a sense of our dependence upon Him we might be motivated to seek after Him. To acknowledge God in all our ways is part of the reverence which intelligent and dependent creatures owe to the supreme Creator and Governor of all. This provides us with hope that He will direct our paths. But if we neglect this, we'll have no right to expect the guidance and blessing of heaven. We should not then be surprised to meet with disappointment and grief. God alone knows all the temptations and difficulties, advantages and disadvantages, we face in life, and our abilities to bear them. He has often directed those who honestly seek His direction onto a path that brings contentment and happiness.

5. Consistent with what has been discussed, one's personal preferences should also be considered. For example, when someone is very much interested in a particular calling, this may indicate a direction of providence and, thus, help us move toward making a proper choice. People generally are best at, and most easily bear the inconveniences associated with, those employments and situations to which they are naturally inclined.

One should consider meditating on the following Scripture verses when seeking their calling:

"I would seek unto God, and unto God would I commit my cause." (Job 5:8).

"Then I proclaimed a fast there, at the river of Ahava, that we might afflict ourselves before our God, to seek of him a right way for us, and for our little ones, and for all our substance. So we fasted and besought our God for this: and he was entreated of us." (Ezra 8:21,23).

"O our God, wilt thou not judge them? for we have no might

OF CHOOSING A CALLING

against this great company that cometh against us; neither know we what to do: but our eyes are upon thee." (2 Chronicles 20:12).

"Where no counsel is, the people fall: but in the multitude of counsellors there is safety." (Proverbs 11:14).

"Trust in the LORD with all thine heart; and lean not unto thine own understanding. Be not wise in thine own eyes: fear the LORD, and depart from evil." (Proverbs 3:5,7).

"A man's heart deviseth his way: but the LORD directeth his steps." (Proverbs 16:9).

"O LORD, I know that the way of man is not in himself: it is not in man that walketh to direct his steps." (Jeremiah 10:23).

"And let ours also learn to maintain good works for necessary uses, that they be not unfruitful." (Titus 3:14).

"Let him that stole steal no more: but rather let him labour, working with his hands the thing which is good, that he may have to give to him that needeth." (Ephesians 4:28).

"Woe unto him that buildeth his house by unrighteousness, and his chambers by wrong; that useth his neighbour's service without wages, and giveth him not for his work." (Jeremiah 22:13).

"And if ye walk contrary unto me, and will not hearken unto me; I will bring seven times more plagues upon you according to your sins. Then I will walk contrary unto you also in fury; and I, even I, will chastise you seven times for your sins." (Leviticus 26:21,28).

"Wealth gotten by vanity shall be diminished: but he that gathereth by labour shall increase." (Proverbs 13:11).

"Treasures of wickedness profit nothing: but righteousness delivereth from death." (Proverbs 10:2).

"He that soweth iniquity shall reap vanity: and the rod of his anger shall fail." (Proverbs 22:8).

Proper Motivation of Faith

It was mentioned earlier that one needs to consider the individual's personal interests and views when selecting a means of employment. Since we are beings not governed by instinct, as irrational creatures are, but are given reasoning abilities by God so that we may use them, we should first consider the motives we have for doings things and the manner in which we do them. We certainly should be seeking after that which agrees with what God has instructed us to do and how to do them, so that we might be worthy of the reasoning abilities given us. Thus, it's very important that our minds be influenced and directed by our faith. The problems that many people have may be rightly attributed to their lack of exposure to sound advice and religion. They may go to universities or go into trades without any sense of responsibilities or dangers and, being unprepared, are soon surprised and overcome by the many evil temptations in the world. To prevent this, seek after a true understanding of the Christian faith, and regulate your tempers and conduct accordingly in every aspect of life.

1. *Let a sincere love and reverence of God, and the desire for His acceptance and favor through Christ Jesus, be the guiding principle and motive for all you do.* When the mind is devoted to God, and turned to pleasing Him, we're provided with the best defense against error and recklessness today, as well as misery and penalty tomorrow. If we sincerely serve God, He will surely bless us. He will interest Himself in our concerns, and support us in our difficulties. He will give us the direction of His wisdom, the comfort of His grace, and keep us from a multitude of foolishness and miseries, things which overtake those who are motivated by worldly gain or their own lusts and vicious appetites.

OF CHOOSING A CALLING

To help you do this, consider the following guidelines:

Know that it is in your best interest, as well as your duty, to come to a true and early faith in Christ. It is for this that you have been created and redeemed, that your life continues to be maintained, and which God claims is His due. Do the things related to your calling, "Not with eyeservice, as menpleasers; but as the servants of Christ, doing the will of God from the heart; With good will doing service, as to the Lord, and not to men." (Ephesians 6:6-7). This will bring dignity to the least noble work, help you fulfill your calling and find happiness, whatever success you might find in other matters.

2. *As you depend upon the help of God, let your faith in Christ be based on sound principles.* Temptations and difficulties that were unknown to you before will now appear in every new area of life. This can quickly overcome those who are unprepared or uncertain. However, if you are quick to discern that which exists beneath the surface and remain aware of the temptations and consequences of evil, by the grace of the Lord Jesus Christ, you may escape them.

Of all temptations to which young people may be exposed, none is more destructive and deadly than evil company. Such company is found everywhere which, like the fallen angels in rebellion against God, attempts to draw others into the same guilt and condemnation they bear. Therefore, never begin friendships with others until you have received a positive report on their character from a reliable source or you have spent a sufficient amount of time observing them yourself so as to be confident of their good character. Don't rely only on former acquaintances when you're considering new friendships, for someone may have appeared very innocent earlier in their life but now be very wicked and cruel. Likewise, just because someone appears to be smart, well educated, or has come from a good family, don't become attached to them if their life is not one with a serious faith and strict virtues. The further one is from such a life, the more dangerous they are likely to be. You must be discerning in these matters. If, as part of coming to know someone, their conversation continues to reveal ungodly characteristics, you should consider ending the relationship. Be careful because, once you become entangled with evil company, it can become difficult for you to break off the relationship. If you have to communicate with people of questionable character, such as for business purposes, do so at a sensible distance. And if you find yourself wavering on the relationship, and your spiritual zeal begin to wane because of it, go to the Word of God to see what He says you should do. Then consider, which is the best path for you: the judgment of God or that of blind and deluded sinners?

Beware of making a false profession of holiness and virtue, characteristics that are vitally important to a real and practical faith in Christ. Consider whether, on the Day of Judgment, such people will not curse themselves for their vain profession, for neglecting the faith they now sinfully mock. Think about whether those who forsake God, their responsibilities and best interests, by maintaining close relationships with the ungodly, should deserve to perish. Seek after those who are prudent, wise and faithful to God, and build relationships with them. "He that walketh with wise men shall be wise: but a companion of fools shall be destroyed." (Proverbs 13:20).

Maintain a discerning nature not only with the regular business of your callings but with the difficulties as well. In time, such discernment will help you to overcome new struggles. When we exercise our bodies and minds, they're strengthened and improved, making it easier and more enjoyable to do those things we once most dreaded. As you learn this, determine to continue to overcome any difficulties. Don't become discouraged when you meet with large, unknown obstacles. Don't let them bring you to anger or harsh words. Divine providence permits such things to keep us humble and to tame those desires common to youth. Therefore, patiently and cheerfully submit to such troubles in your calling, while continuing to hope that peace and satisfaction will overcome toil and trouble.

3. Let me particularly recommend that you always be humble and faithful, knowing that, because of this, you'll be highly esteemed and respected for this by those you work with and by others who come to know you. Humility will bring ease and contentment to everything you do in life. It will help you to work well with others, be easily pleased yet hard to provoke, and generally appreciated. Those who are humble believe all the good they receive to be more than they deserve. They don't think themselves above the most menial tasks as part of honest employment, nor do they neglect having both a sincere and respectful behavior toward others.

Likewise, don't be one who worries or argues about when to obey, or become envious of those you should respect, or dislike those you should embrace. Such attitudes are the consequence of a prideful heart, which is a disposition that will turn you against God, as well as make you disrespectful of men and uneasy with yourself. Every effort will become too burdensome, every criticism too irritating, and every week become as a year. Then the time will come when that work will end but, as long as one is enslaved to their pride and passions, they'll carry this bad attitude with them wherever they go.

Fidelity (or faithfulness) is another desirable trait that you should develop. Be true and sincere in what you say. Stay far away from lying and pretending, which are vices that are destructive to all friendships and relationships between men. Such characteristics of people destroy the mutual confidence so needed in society. So, be determined at all times and in all situations to speak the truth whatever it may cost you.

When one confesses their faults honestly, they will more quickly be forgiven and preserve their good character than when they seek to excuse or deny them, which at best will only cover them up for a moment. Let your fidelity extend to your deeds as well as your words. Always be punctual and just in everything that is entrusted to you. Hold those you work with in high esteem and do not divulge any secrets about them, regardless of the reason. Then, although you may not always perform up to their expectations, your faithfulness to them will bring you their love and respect.

An honest heart compensates for other weaknesses that you might have. Natural weaknesses may be pitied and forgiven, but unfaithfulness and deceit are exceedingly disliked by both God and man. Therefore, whatever responsibilities and temptations you might have, always be honest and truthful. Never imagine that your skills or abilities can compensate for their absence.

4. Let the study of the sacred Scriptures always occupy some part of your leisure time. They are your surest guide to responsibilities and finding happiness. There the mind of the blessed God is revealed to man, to protect him from the worst of evils, to direct him to the highest good, and to show man the thoughts of His heart towards him forever.

Some parts of Scripture abound with the most fascinating histories, which are highly instructive because they not only describe the activities of men but the motivations behind them, free from all fiction and falsehood. Here we are presented with a system of the highest morality, founded upon the most rational and exalted concepts of God, and enforced by the most awesome and interesting authority. They're admirably designed by God to heal the conscience, to purify, to comfort, to exhort the soul, to inspire

OF CHOOSING A CALLING

it with principles of virtue and goodness, and to strengthen and confirm it in practice. In short, they're able to make us wise unto salvation through faith in Christ Jesus. When your mind comes to be delighted in the pleasure and the purity of Scripture, it will become less necessary to caution you against becoming attracted to the loose and immoral writings that are so common today. Although famous for their wit and politeness, the writings of today tend to poison the heart, corrupt beliefs, and corrupt the affections. In return for one beneficial lesson, they are filled with a thousand harmful ones.

5. Let humble and earnest prayer to God for His grace and favor be the constant breath of your souls. Never think that good intentions will protect you from moral evil, nor your labor and skill from natural evil, if they're without the blessing of heaven that comes through prayer. Without this, success cannot be ensured, even with the best materials, the wisest instructors and the most profitable activities. Frequent failure by those who otherwise showed the most promise plainly reveals that God stands by His call for men to come to Him in prayer. Whatever advantages men may have, they are all but meaningless without God's blessings that come by no other way.

This is important not only when a new business begins but throughout all seasons of life, for we constantly need to depend upon God for continuing blessings both now and in the future. Morning and evening prayer is the key to opening God's mercy during the day and shutting out dangers during the night. Therefore, you should be constantly and sincerely in prayer, remaining grateful as God blesses you, remembering "If I regard iniquity in my heart, the Lord will not hear me." (Psalm 66:18).

Thus, having chosen a lawful calling, having your mind influenced by the principles given in Scripture and by God's grace having grown in practicing sound faith, you may comfortably and vigorously pursue that which is required by your callings. To assist you in doing this are the following verses of Scripture.

SCRIPTURE REFERENCES FOR CHAPTER 2

"O that there were such an heart in them, that they would fear me, and keep all my commandments always, that it might be well with them, and with their children for ever! Ye shall walk in all the ways which the LORD your God hath commanded you, that ye may live, and that it may be well with you, and that ye may prolong your days in the land which ye shall possess." (Deuteronomy 5:29,33).

"Now therefore fear the LORD, and serve him in sincerity and in truth: and put away the gods which your fathers served on the other side of the flood, and in Egypt; and serve ye the LORD. And the people answered and said, God forbid that we should forsake the LORD, to serve other gods." (Joshua 24:14,16).

"What man is he that desireth life, and loveth many days, that he may see good? Depart from evil, and do good; seek peace, and pursue it." (Psalm 34:12,14).

"My son, if sinners entice thee, consent thou not. My son, walk not thou in the way with them; refrain thy foot from their path." (Proverbs 1:10,15).

"My son, forget not my law; but let thine heart keep my commandments: For length of days, and long life, and peace, shall they add to thee. Let not mercy and truth forsake thee: bind them about thy neck; write them upon the table of thine heart: So shalt thou find favour and good understanding in the sight of God and man." (Proverbs 3:1-4).

"Wisdom is the principal thing; therefore get wisdom: and with all thy getting get understanding. Exalt her, and she shall promote thee: she shall bring thee to honour, when thou dost embrace her. She shall give to thine head an ornament of grace: a

OF CHOOSING A CALLING

crown of glory shall she deliver to thee. Take fast hold of instruction; let her not go: keep her; for she is thy life. Enter not into the path of the wicked, and go not in the way of evil men. Avoid it, pass not by it, turn from it, and pass away. Ponder the path of thy feet, and let all thy ways be established." (Proverbs 4:7-9, 13-15, 26).

"And thou, Solomon my son, know thou the God of thy father, and serve him with a perfect heart and with a willing mind: for the LORD searcheth all hearts, and understandeth all the imaginations of the thoughts: if thou seek him, he will be found of thee; but if thou forsake him, he will cast thee off for ever." (1 Chronicles 28:9).

"For our rejoicing is this, the testimony of our conscience, that in simplicity and godly sincerity, not with fleshly wisdom, but by the grace of God, we have had our conversation in the world, and more abundantly to you-ward." (2 Corinthians 1:12).

"Flee also youthful lusts: but follow righteousness, faith, charity, peace, with them that call on the Lord out of a pure heart." (2 Timothy 2:22).

"Young men likewise exhort to be sober minded." (Titus 2:6).

CHAPTER THREE

Of Prudence and Discretion

*...we should live soberly, righteously,
and godly, in this present world*
TITUS 2:12

THE FIRST THING NECESSARY TO HELP A NEW BUSINESS progress in the right direction is prudence and discretion. With respect to business, such abilities include our handling of matters in the wisest way or, in other words, pursuing the right end, by the best means and in a reasonable timeframe. Here, I'm not referring to a serpent-like craftiness, which lies in wait to take advantage of the unsuspecting, naive or ignorant person, and which teaches men to seek their wealth through unfair or fraudulent means.

God doesn't give superior wisdom or skill to men so that they might use them for purposes that are contrary to his will and the general good of mankind.

THEIR NATURE AND ADVANTAGES

Here, we are referring to the kind of honest wisdom that is not only consistent with a good conscience but actually enhances it. To be prudent is to avoid the kind of wrong or unwarranted behaviors that can corrupt wisdom. Wisdom, like light, is pleasant to behold. It quickens the spirits, leads to a cheerful attitude, and brings clarity and honesty to life. It benefits us in other ways as well, and frees us from many potential evils and difficulties. For example, we find wisdom to be associated with sound advice, educated insight, stable decisions, and orderly behavior. It helps prevent evils that may occur from blind ignorance, false presumption, gullibility, impulsive behavior, and inconsistencies in setting goals. Wisdom gives us a sense of calm and hope of success.

To man God has given a thoughtful mind, sagacity and foresight, which He has denied to other creatures. Still, there are those who resemble the beasts by their foolish and disgraceful behavior. Many are destroyed by such behavior. However, when we do with good intentions that which is appropriate, we can reasonably hope to be blessed and be doubly pleased when we are successful. In such cases, even when complete success doesn't come, we'll at least know that it was not due to our own foolishness. We're not suggesting that our wisdom and prudence have any control over divine providence or make unnecessary our dependence upon God. But it will keep us from being our own worst enemies. It's the means by which the great Governor of the world uses to give us prosperity and happiness, and grants us enjoyment of them. Finally, although success is more often the product of a thoughtful mind than the labor of hands, success in business is frequently the result of the two working together.

THEIR APPLICATION

Now that we've considered the nature and advantages of prudence and discretion, we can focus on those activities where the tradesman is called to apply it. I'll describe a few examples.

1. *In helping to fully understand his calling, by increasing his knowledge of the different ways and methods associated with it.* For example, in his calling the tradesman needs to understand the nature and quality of the products he deals in, when and

OF PRUDENCE AND DISCRETION

where to buy and sell them, the number of products, the best manufacturing methods and skills, and those certain "secrets" that are common to most callings and on which success often depends. He needs to study and understand these and all other aspects of the business. Let others be concerned with knowing about unrelated callings or be prying into the matters and work of others. Remember that "The wisdom of the prudent is to understand his way: but the folly of fools is deceit." (Proverbs 14:8). Your trade or calling is what you need to focus on. Spend your time on improving your mind and aptitude. Neither God nor man will condemn you for inexperience in regard to the business of others. Always be learning how to utilize your time wisely. Continue to gain knowledge by observation and instruction, and be willing to learn new useful skills. Remember that the lack of knowledge can be detrimental to success even when the circumstances are very much in your favor. Such businesses might be likened to a rich vessel guided by an unskilled pilot in danger of being shipwrecked and lost. On the other hand, every masterful tradesman should carefully, honestly and faithfully instruct their apprentices in all of the lawful and useful details of their callings. They should do this as a matter of justice and honor, as well as by any agreements between them.

2. *In making wise choices that are inherent to trade.*

For time

Make choices based on that which is most appropriate to your business. Remember, "To every thing there is a season, and a time to every purpose under the heaven" (Ecclesiastes 3:1). In addition, every wise businessman will note that there is a time to buy and a time to sell. Every business must plan for future uncertainties and variations in the value of their products, including the impact of various uncertainties and unknowns. It is important to attempt to buy goods when they are cheap and sell them when they're in demand. At all times avoid buying goods when their price is too high or volatile. The future is unknown to us but the benefits from making good business decisions are known, and those who are discriminating and wise are most likely to be successful.

For Place

It is prudent for the businessman to consider that which is most suitable and proper for his calling. It is important that he use good judgment when choosing between the needs of his family and the needs of his business. The proper balance between the two may be very appropriate for one type of employment but different for another. However, regardless of the financial condition of the family, whether you own an upscale house or rent a more modest place, one cannot avoid the necessity of finding and keeping customers.

For Persons

Much prudence is necessary regarding the persons one does business with. First is the question of whom to trust, for it is not the metal that glitters most that is always the richest. That is, many men in business are deceitful, and seek to enrich themselves by exploiting those who are naive or gullible. Therefore, it is always a good idea to first look into the backgrounds of others before putting our trust in them. Certainly, there is prudence in trusting some and charity in trusting others. However, there are many whom it is neither prudent nor charitable to trust at all. Deal only with men of conscience or, at least, of common honesty, for they're more reliable than others. It's always better to work with men of good character than with unprincipled men. A general understanding of others can be determined by their reputation.

OF PRUDENCE AND DISCRETION

Finally, there is the question of who you should become familiar with. Although we should be friendly toward all, we usually can be very familiar with only a few. These few should include those with whom we have a mutually beneficial business relationship. There won't be too many such relationships, for the tradesman's employment won't allow him sufficient time to develop close relationships with very many. Choose those who are wise and prudent, virtuous and good, for nothing has a greater influence on our current or future well-being than our close relationships, It has been observed, "He that walketh with wise men shall be wise: but a companion of fools shall be destroyed." (Proverbs 13:20).

3. Prudence should be part of making every important decision. There are many cases where even clever men have been destroyed by their hastiness. This happens when one doesn't sufficiently consider both the circumstances and the consequences necessary to keeping them headed in the right direction. Instead, they suddenly head off in the wrong direction because of something that appears to be reasonable, only to do permanent harm to themselves and their families. Often, their actions are guided by their imaginations or infatuations, rather than by reason and discernment. Others miss potentially beneficial opportunities through worry or neglect that interferes with the timely keeping of goals.

Therefore, one needs to give appropriate attention to the matter at hand, depending on its importance and difficulty, and the amount of time available. If the situation permits, spend an evening thinking it over. Doing this and then reviewing everything in the morning will help you come to the right decision. Of course, with regard to trivial decisions, it would be foolish and unnecessary to spend a great deal of time on them. However, as with all decisions, it's better to be overly cautious in both word and deed than to be too hasty.

4. *In matching your abilities to the needs of your business.*

Of Mind

Don't over-burden your abilities or gifts. Like a spring that has been over-stretched, the mind of a man can lose it strength. A ship that is well-built, rigged and balanced will carry a heavy load. But, if it's over-loaded, it will sink. Similarly, some have greater abilities or gifts than others, but all have their limitations. Therefore, when you become so over-burdened with business as to become unfit for the service of God, no longer enjoy what you're doing, or when you can neither eat nor sleep, nor be cheerful, nor pray, its time to take a break from your work.

Of Body

Don't undertake any work that is beyond your own strength. When this happens, it's usually the result of much greed, that is, a desire to have everything. This is something that can make men slaves in their callings. The result is that either those who employ them become disappointed or they hurt themselves. In the latter case, their own peace of mind can be disturbed and their health and strength can be impaired. We should never forget to spend time and effort on spiritual matters, remembering that our bodies were designed to be the temples of the Holy Ghost and not laborers and slaves to the world. Nor should we forget that vanity and greed are often at the root of sinful lives.

Of Estate

Always seek to keep your feet on the ground. Although in some cases, where the probability for success is very high or certain, it may be acceptable, even prudent, for someone to expand their business beyond what they initially established or contemplated.

OF PRUDENCE AND DISCRETION

Still, every wise man should be very cautious when considering doing this. I don't see how any honest man, accountable before God and his own conscience, would consider such a venture unless they had first notified and gotten some form of encouragement from those who might have helped them establish their business financially. In such cases one might ask themselves: What right do I have for taking financial help from others and perhaps endangering it?

Common motives for financially hazardous enterprises are pride and greed. Every prudent tradesman should be watching out for such things, for as the water may be sufficient for one watermill, it may barely be enough for two. Similarly, the assistance that one person may cheerfully provide for a small business may turn into confusion and anxiety when they become financially burdened. Such stories often end sadly. He that was not content with his business as it was may need to be content to live upon another's charity.

5. *In regulating your expenses according to your abilities.* On the one hand, men should not intentionally live so far below their incomes, perhaps because of a sour disposition, that they deprive themselves and their families of certain necessities of life. On the other hand, they should be very cautious to keep their expenses under control. It isn't prophetic to predict the unhappy consequences of excessive spending. Expensive living is a kind of slow fever that preys upon the spirits and lives of those in business. It can grow to such a point that it endangers the business itself. It feeds upon the two most important aspects of a man's trade: his credit and his cash. Eventually, the financially weakened businessman becomes overwhelmed.

There can be times when the temper of the nation becomes very full of itself, where the people are driven to excessive spending, which I think may very properly be called a plague upon them. The poor try to live like the rich, and the rich like the great, and the great like the greatest. A nation can become diverted in this way for a while.

Some people are such slaves to their appetites that they spend everything for which their head and hands have worked. Some people develop pride in their expensive houses and furniture or in costly clothes for themselves, their wives, or their children. Others indulge in many luxurious forms of entertainment or don't take care of the things they have, motivating others to speak out against their wasteful extravagance. Many are continually ruined by an excessive love of pleasure, with all of its associated costs. Many a tradesman will discover that his determination won't be enough to withstand this torrent of evil. However, prudence will teach him to live below rather than above his income, not knowing what losses and frustrations the future may bring.

6. *It is prudent for the tradesman to frequently review the state of his business, so that he may know its financial status.* First, this is important to our souls which, if neglected, can be harmful to us spiritually. It is important temporally as well. To this end, your bookkeeping should include an ability to get a quick and accurate financial picture of your business. When you do this and you find your business improving, then you should be satisfied and pleased, and motivated to give thanks to God for His goodness in blessing your labor. If you find things to be at a standstill, you'll want to find ways to be more thrifty and productive as soon as possible. And if the books tell you that your business is declining, you'll want to determine its cause and examine where you might make improvements.

In the latter case above, you should especially try to determine whether the reason for your financial difficulty has been the result of any unlawful behavior towards God, neglect of the

OF PRUDENCE AND DISCRETION

Sabbath or worship, or uncharitableness to the poor or injustice to others. "If ye will not hear, and if ye will not lay it to heart, to give glory unto my name, saith the LORD of hosts, I will even send a curse upon you, and I will curse your blessings: yea, I have cursed them already, because ye do not lay it to heart." (Malachi 2:2). Therefore, take a good hard look at your conduct before God and man when such things happen. Inspect the state of your business affairs, for it's better for you to review your own accounts than to have the government officials do it for you. Let me give you this bit of advice. If you find things going so poorly that you're unable to satisfy any creditors, it's both prudent and just that you consider ending the business you might have. It will at least help you maintain your good reputation as an honest man. You may even find your creditors willing to assist you in future enterprises.

7. Use prudence to direct those passions to which our callings make us most vulnerable. The passions of the mind are natural to us, and inseparable from us. But how we manage them and keep them in check is the business of wisdom and virtue. To be a servant to them is worse them becoming a slave. This is a danger for the tradesman, which has various causes. For example, it can occur in the form of discontentment if his merchandise does not sell well or, for some reason, there are problems in making them. He may become envious as he thinks about others who appear to be achieving more prosperity or success in some way. Then there are situations where he might develop unjustified fears because of a natural inclination to avoid certain evils, which can cause his mental state to fluctuate and his spirits to sink. It is prudent to eliminate such excessive fears.

When we do what we should be doing and act according to our best judgment, we shouldn't let ourselves become greatly disturbed by events in the world but, rather, put our faith in the wise and good providence of God. Still, foolish hope is often more fatal to the concerns of men than groundless fears. At least our fears can help us strengthen ourselves spiritually in anticipation of certain evils. But foolish hope often gives us a false and fatal sense of security.

How many tradesmen have been ruined by their vain hope! A get-rich scheme can appear attractive from a distance, but will lead a man through numerous difficulties during their pursuit. However, when he takes a closer look at it, it vanishes into air. Others develop great expectations regarding the death of rich friends or some other uncertain scenario. As a result, they begin to neglect their business, live beyond their means, and eventually give up what they already have only to chase after mere shadows. This often happens even when one realizes he's already sinking. He props up his spirits with such foolish hopes until he reaches a point where he can neither avoid falling nor recover from it.

Another passion that's all too common to the tradesman is a tendency to be quickly or easily angered. Such a character flaw is often revealed, more or less, by his natural temper and by his work. Wisdom and prudence can help suppress it. A wise man, before he gives in to anger, will consider whether there's sufficient cause for it or whether it's likely to have a positive effect. He'll make allowances for the circumstances of the situation and the people involved, avoiding any expressions of resentment until he has calmed down. He does this so that his decisions may be just and merciful and his anger not sinful.

Some customers can be annoying, some workers idle and untrustworthy, and some relatives rowdy and cranky. However, such matters won't disturb the peace of mind of the tradesman who is spiritually wise and prudent, nor confuse his business dealings, nor cause him to be rude or disrespectful to his customers. Here is a maxim with certainty: the more we are governed by

OF PRUDENCE AND DISCRETION

wisdom, the less we shall be inflamed by passion.

8. Discretion should be prudently used when considering the many unforeseen events of our callings. Such events are inherently of great variety and can occur during any of the tradesman's activities. The prudent man will pay attention to what is happening in this or that country, or in this or the other commodity, gathering information from various reliable sources, and then ordering his business affairs accordingly. If every trade had a definite and consistent method and order of events, one might be able to get by with relatively little business sense. However, this is not the case for most trades.

It is also necessary for us to draw upon our reasoning abilities, as well as our observations and experience, to help us decide when to expand or reduce our sales, and what course to take. We should always remember to behave in a just and charitable way toward others. We should never seek to utilize our insight and knowledge to influence and entrap those who might be somewhat naive or immature.

On the other hand, some things are beyond our control. We should consider that which is before us today to be our responsibility, but that which is in the future to be in God's hands. Whatever disappointments we meet with in our callings, we should always patiently and cheerfully submit to His wisdom and government, continue to trust in His goodness, take care of our responsibilities, and be diligent in our work. And, as we do this, we should maintain the hope that any losses we might have incurred will be recovered for the peace and enjoyment of our own minds, or by the blessings of divine providence, or both.

9. Prudence should be especially utilized in avoiding those situations in which others have been ruined. Every failing tradesman provides a kind of object lesson for us, as we remember that it's far better to learn wisdom from the mistakes of others than our own. Look beyond your own business and become aware of the reasons for the failures of other business and their circumstances. Avoid making their mistakes. Let's look at a few examples.

Company Keeping

Here, I am considering the matter not from a religious view but from a view of being cautious. From this latter view, we see how often an excess of social activities has harmed the business of the tradesman. Business neglected is business lost. So the tradesman who is satisfied with being away from his business all the time has no right to expect it to succeed. Time spent away from business necessarily takes time and money from the business. The loss in time is often more fatal than loss of money, since money can be recovered but time cannot. During the time that one is away from work, business opportunities arise, important customers come to buy and, not finding the owner, go elsewhere. Unexpected bargains may become available for sale, opportunities that may never return. Workers can be left to themselves who, if they are unfaithful and careless, wind up stealing the cash, chasing away customers, and damaging or even destroying the merchandise.

Although it may appear odd at first, there's no doubt that the damage can be just as great even when the workers are hardworking, cooperative and faithful. For example, a worker who used to act as shop manager while the owner was away may at some point choose to establish his own shop, which will necessarily draw customers from that business to him. So, the man who was satisfied with the shadow of authority in his shop may come to find the shadow of a business when he returns, after his clever shop manager leaves. Therefore, let your attendance in the business be ongoing, your products good, the prices reasonable,

OF PRUDENCE AND DISCRETION

and your behavior acceptable.

I may venture to suggest that, with the blessing of providence, you'll be more successful following these principles than spending all your time away from your business along with its associated expenses and the neglect of your workers and your family. There is an even worse consequence to the wasted time and money, which is all too often overlooked: the loss of the soul that can occur from the influences of corrupt principles and evil practices. They that are least sensible of their danger in this respect are most likely to feel its fatal effects.

Suretyship

This refers to a tradesman who agrees to have his business used as financial security for someone else's business, often because he anticipates it will benefit his own business. Although some believe this may be lawful, and in some cases even necessary, in all cases it requires the utmost care and caution. We should never enter into financial obligations in our business unless we are able to satisfy them without injuring our families and ourselves or causing mental distress, and unless we can fulfill them as with all other financial obligations. Should one provide security for others, they should do so according to both law and conscience, understanding the great risks should the principal become bankrupt.

If the situation is so dire that one believes a business cannot operate with financial surety from someone else, I have the following comment. Although there may be a limit in the size a business can attain without it, the reason for wanting to grow can be one of pride and greed, and end in disaster. There are ways that the business may continue or even expand in a way that is safer and more comfortable. If the person is a man of prudence and integrity, the creditor may agree to rely on his guarantee alone, without involving another party. If that is not the case, then you shouldn't put your trust in him either.

If your refusal to enter into financial obligations like this cause you to lose a friendship or their gratitude, consider other ways that you might help them. For example, try to convince them that your decision wasn't based on a lack of respect or friendship toward them. If an individual, it may be that he is already too deeply indebted to you or others financially. Perhaps he is simply less careful and just than you imagine. And, given the reality that he is mortal as we all are, you may rightly be concerned that his estate would only entangle you with problems, some of which might be disastrous to you. These are not merely unfounded possibilities, but things that happen every day. Therefore, "My son, if thou be surety for thy friend, if thou hast stricken thy hand with a stranger, Thou art snared with the words of thy mouth, thou art taken with the words of thy mouth. Do this now, my son, and deliver thyself, when thou art come into the hand of thy friend; go, humble thyself, and make sure thy friend. Give not sleep to thine eyes, nor slumber to thine eyelids. Deliver thyself as a roe from the hand of the hunter, and as a bird from the hand of the fowler." (Proverbs 6:1-5).

Gaming

Prudence will also help to keep you from certain ruinous practices and activities. Many people spend a lot of time in gaming activities. Here, I'm not suggesting that an occasional game of cards or other similar activity will always cause men to neglect the spiritual lives of themselves and their families. My principal concern are those games of risk that are not so much a diversion but a business, who come to depend upon their success at it in a way that cannot be justified by reason or conscience. Make it a rule to never play such games for money. A better rule would be to avoid such games altogether.

Although there are many other vices that can be harmful to

OF PRUDENCE AND DISCRETION

you, these two, (sureties and gaming) can destroy you. Because of them, many have, within a relatively short time, financially bankrupted themselves and their families beyond their ability to recover. Therefore, don't let the lure of quick profits put you on a path that is contrary to God's laws, and harm to your friendships and love for others. Instead, determine to never consider any get-rich-quick schemes. "Enter not into the path of the wicked, and go not in the way of evil men. Avoid it, pass not by it, turn from it, and pass away." (Proverbs 4:14-15). Never consider your wealth your own until you've either restored or returned all that you've gained through dishonesty or by injury to others.

Prudence will help you avoid an excessive curiosity or tendency to meddle in the concerns of others. Every tradesman has enough business at home to occupy his time and efforts, either in works of piety to God, charity to the needy, graciousness toward friends and family, or the necessary tasks associated with his calling. Without a just cause and an invitation, it's unwise to be meddling in the affairs of others. Usually, much time is lost and little good is accomplished. Above all, be very careful in regard to getting involved with affairs of state.

Many people allow themselves to waste a lot of their time on the business of others. Some seek to obtain a profound knowledge of politics or become familiar with private discussions or secret political schemes to which they often add rash criticisms of things they really don't understand. Some people seem to always be trying to find fault with those in civil government. They're able to note who was responsible for everything that has gone wrong, or whose pride or revenge was served when this or that step was taken or new law made. When they do this, not only are they being foolish but they're also diverting others from what they should be doing, from what's most prudent and necessary. They thereby serve to stir up rebellious behavior.

You should make an effort to fulfill the position in which you

THE RELIGIOUS TRADESMAN

are placed by doing what you're called to do, and to promote the public good by all prudent and praiseworthy means. Don't let good intentions or your personal expectations or any kind of worry cause you to disturb the public peace, to dishonor your rulers, or to do anything unlawful. Let God alone rule according to His sovereignty. Let lawful magistrates alone rule their subjects. And let it be your business to cheerfully obey or quietly suffer. "If ye be reproached for the name of Christ, happy are ye; for the spirit of glory and of God resteth upon you: on their part he is evil spoken of, but on your part he is glorified. But let none of you suffer as a murderer, or as a thief, or as an evildoer, or as a busybody in other men's matters." (1 Peter 4:14-15).

10 . *Prudence will help you to arrange the common affairs of life so as not to interfere with spiritual responsibilities in a way that they harmonize and assist each other.* It's true that some types of work and the requirements placed on some tradesmen allow them less time for worshipping God and devotions than others. But, regardless of the details behind the reason, the pious tradesman will find some time to spend on spiritual matters. He won't focus so hard on the things of this world as to forget the eternal concerns of another world. His devotional time helps to bring order to his business, and so his business welcomes the time he gives to devotions. The less time he is able to spare during the week for devotions, the more attention he should give to the Christian Sabbath when it arrives. In this way, he works to receive the blessing of heaven on all the labors of life. He gains wisdom and virtue which helps him fulfill his responsibilities and bear the burdens that go along with them. However, if he isn't prudent and avoids his spiritual responsibilities, he may come to develop a distaste for devotions. He may become confused about how to properly spend time in devotions, which he would find to be a time of much delight and benefit if it were prudently and sincerely performed.

Conclusion

In conclusion, from what has been said, we've learned about how prudence is important to the tradesman. It may be of more benefit to him than everything he owns or all his friends. It will make him well liked and useful to others, and happy with himself as well. Therefore, we should be interested in obtaining as much of this excellent character quality, prudence, as possible. It's true that it's a natural gift, and all men don't seem to be equally gifted with it.

As with any ability of the mind, there are ways that it may be improved. It may be helpful to spend time studying the causes and consequences associated with various events. Seek to understand any biases you might have that could influence your decision-making abilities. Learn to take time to weigh the different issues before making your decisions in proportion to the importance or difficulty of the matter. The reason why I bring this up is because I find that people often make careless decisions, not because they are unable to judge the nature or consequences of the matter but because of their enthusiasm and haste. Men wind up doing that which they would not do if they only took the time to think through everything in a cool and mature way.

Consider the people and things involved in order for you to gain wisdom. Let your observations of every thriving or decaying tradesman be a lesson to you. Solomon learned wisdom in a way you should imitate: "I went by the field of the slothful, and by the vineyard of the man void of understanding; And, lo, it was all grown over with thorns, and nettles had covered the face thereof, and the stone wall thereof was broken down. Then I saw, and considered it well: I looked upon it, and received instruction." (Proverbs 24:30-32).

Consult wise men. If you're willing to learn, you'll want to spend time observing the ways of others. Don't think that you're able to instantly grasp every principle and rule associated with wisdom and prudence. Instead, choose to spend time learning among the wise rather than priding yourself among the foolish. "The way of a fool is right in his own eyes: but he that hearkeneth unto counsel is wise." (Proverbs 12:15).

Be sure to study the sacred Scriptures. They are the words of the only wise God. There you'll find precepts of wisdom suited to every state and condition of life, particularly in the Book of Proverbs, which was dictated by the Spirit of God "To give subtilty to the simple, to the young man knowledge and discretion." (Proverbs 1:4). Proverbs is a book that should be consulted often by every religious tradesman. Even the world would prefer it to the writings of Socrates, Seneca, or Cicero if they were not biased against words of Divine inspiration.

Pray that the Father of truth would instruct you, "For the LORD giveth wisdom: out of his mouth cometh knowledge and understanding." (Proverbs 2:6). And, "If any of you lack wisdom, let him ask of God, that giveth to all men liberally, and upbraideth not; and it shall be given him." (James 1:5). God knows all relationships between things. He can influence our minds and direct our thoughts. He can save you from fatal errors in any area of life, and keep away temptations from you. God can give more wisdom that man can get by himself. Those who most seriously and constantly depend on Him are certainly the people most likely to have wisdom of the type that God Himself will approve.

What I'm recommending is the development of an honest and worthy habit of prudence, not that which is reduced to something that is secondary or merely a craft. Don't be one who, under the pretence of wisdom, tries to impress or deceive others, or take advantage of the innocence or good intentions of their neighbors for purposes of their own greed or ambitions. Such pretence is wisdom from below and, since it comes from hell, it leads some back to it, "Know ye not that the unrighteous shall not inherit the kingdom of God? Be not deceived: neither fornicators, nor idolaters, nor adulterers, nor effeminate, nor abusers of themselves with mankind," (1 Corinthians 6:9). This plainly implies that it is more than merely possible for the prospect of gain to blind the minds of men, to make them seemingly unaware of their guilt and danger. Whatever uneasiness such persons may have of their own insightfulness and prudence, the world cannot produce a greater fool than he that will insult God, injure his neighbor, and destroy his own soul, all for the sake of monetary gain.

Scripture References for Chapter 3

"A good man sheweth favour, and lendeth: he will guide his affairs with discretion." (Psalm 112:5).

"My son, attend unto my wisdom, and bow thine ear to my understanding: That thou mayest regard discretion, and that thy lips may keep knowledge." (Proverbs 5:1-2).

"I wisdom dwell with prudence, and find out knowledge of witty inventions. I lead in the way of righteousness, in the midst of the paths of judgment: That I may cause those that love me to inherit substance; and I will fill their treasures." (Proverbs 8:12,20-21).

"In the lips of him that hath understanding wisdom is found: but a rod is for the back of him that is void of understanding." (Proverbs 10:13).

"He that troubleth his own house shall inherit the wind: and the fool shall be servant to the wise of heart." (Proverbs 11:29).

"Every prudent man dealeth with knowledge: but a fool layeth open his folly." (Proverbs 13:16).

"Every wise woman buildeth her house: but the foolish

plucketh it down with her hands. The wisdom of the prudent is to understand his way: but the folly of fools is deceit. The simple believeth every word: but the prudent man looketh well to his going." (Proverbs 14:1,8,15).

"There is treasure to be desired and oil in the dwelling of the wise; but a foolish man spendeth it up." (Proverbs 21:20).

"Through wisdom is an house builded; and by understanding it is established: And by knowledge shall the chambers be filled with all precious and pleasant riches." (Proverbs 24:3-4).

"Behold, I send you forth as sheep in the midst of wolves: be ye therefore wise as serpents, and harmless as doves." (Matthew 10:16).

CHAPTER FOUR

Of Diligence

*Whatsoever thy hand findeth
to do, do it with thy might ...*
ECCLESIASTES 9:10

AS APPLIED TO OUR TRADE, DILIGENCE REFERS TO THE habit of applying our minds and bodies in ways consistent with our callings. The result is a reasonable middle ground between laziness and pettiness on the one hand and, on the other, slavish labor and excessive concern. The virtue of diligence is the same for both the religious tradesman and other men. However, in the one case, it comes from what we might call "a better principle" and, therefore, it is directed to "a higher end."

THE CHARACTER OF DILIGENCE

To better understand this, let's consider the character of those who neither know God nor live to Him. Their focus typically centers on themselves. Their guide is their own appetites and desires. But the good man, regardless of his place in life, thinks of himself as the servant of Divine providence. He seeks to honor God, and to follow His Word. He is diligent from both a sense of duty and a desire for God's blessing.

Let's look at a few ways the virtue of diligence is expressed in our lives.

1. As we seriously apply our minds and bodies in our callings. If you're a levelheaded person, one who is discerning or innovative, then you should use those gifts. Although some callings may require such gifts more than others, there is a place for their use in all callings. Whether you're a good organizer, are very energetic, have great physical strength or an inquisitive nature, recognize that those gifts are entrusted to you for service to God.

We're all called to support ourselves through honest labor. Staying busy helps us to use up excess energy, energy that might otherwise be used to serve sinful passions. There is a saying: "the more laborious, the less lascivious." Of course, we're not required to spend all our energy on business activities. Rather, we should use moderation in whatever we do, presenting our labors as acceptable to God. Then, after sufficient food and rest, we'll be ready to apply our gifts and energy once again.

2. In how we apply most of our time in our callings. Just as the servant's time belongs to his master, the master's time belongs to God. Therefore, the religious tradesman will seek to be careful with his use of time, wisely dividing it between the concerns of this life and the next. Think of the hours of time as having wings. Every moment flies up to the Author of time, revealing how we are using it.

The common callings of life necessarily require us to use time wisely. The industrious tradesman will, if health permits, rise early, and have a cheerful attitude in his business. His time will be occupied with his family, his shop, his friends, and perhaps with teaching or learning in the community. The point is that he will not need any help taking time away from that which already seems to be swiftly flying by. "Man goeth forth unto his work and to his labour until the evening." (Psalm 104:23).

OF DILIGENCE

3. Diligence includes being on the lookout for opportunities. Know that great things can be accomplished in a little time. Also, recognize that those who remain alert and diligent are often rewarded with opportunities. If we let such opportunities slip away, they may be gone forever. Remember that, "To every thing there is a season, and a time to every purpose under the heaven." (Ecclesiastes 3:1). Opportunities are like the wind and tide that help men as they sail on their voyage over the seas. Such vigilance is as necessary to success as is labor. Let men be ever so industrious and hardworking, unless they are watchful for good opportunities, their success is likely to be small.

4. In giving attention to details. Over time, that which is small can often turn into something more considerable. For example, the smaller customer can lead the way to larger customers when the former is kept satisfied. This is to say that those who ignore the smaller, seemingly less valuable, things in life can sometimes become prideful and careless, and thereby harm their business. It is wise to remember that, "he who abhors small things shall fall little by little." The bountiful gifts of the Creator when misused by man because of his foolishness and vanity are often then given to someone else who will make better use of them. God forbid that I should encourage a greedy, sordid attitude. What I recommend is that we should always be careful to make the best use of what we have, and to give due regard to the relatively small things upon which greater ones may depend. Many people have benefited from giving constant and careful attention to this. It has helped others, even those with very little, to do far more good than those who are careless yet have a high income. Christ gave us an example when He fed five thousand people with only five loaves and two fishes, showing how easily He could create food while ordering that the fragments be gathered up so that, "When they were filled, he said unto his disciples, Gather up the fragments that remain, that nothing be lost." (John 6:12).

5. *In rejecting activities or hobbies that would divert you from your business.* The tradesman's shop or warehouse should be a place that brings him happiness. He shouldn't be wandering away from it without good reason, for there is his business and source of income. It would need to be something very important to justify his taking a break at some retreat or somewhere else, ignoring his business and family at home. At the shop, employees may have been left to supervise themselves before having a good understanding of how to manage themselves and their time. However, God, by His providence, has entrusted them to be under your authority. If you're the one who will be observing and regulating their behavior, while they continue in your service, you'll be the one held accountable before Him. And, should they develop skills or abilities beyond the work required of them, or become too difficult for you to manage, it may be better for you to let them go than to continue to employ them in a way that may harm someone or be offensive to God. Finally, you should realize that your family will also be weakened if you neglect them.

Paying attention to your business will also help keep you from wasting time and money on entertainment. It may not always be easy to know how much entertainment should be permitted. At the same time, it is apparent that many tradesmen go too far. Many are found spending their time and money at various places of entertainment when they should have been at their shops. Diligence in the business will help minimize the time spent at unnecessary activities. Certainly, some forms of entertainment may be permissible if enjoyed in moderation or on special occasions. However, when they begin to captivate the mind, encroach upon business, or become costly, it is high time to reject or at least restrain them. There is a saying that "diversions should be tasted by us as the dogs of Egypt are said to do with the water of the Nile, with great caution lest the crocodiles devour them."

Needless and fruitless trips will be minimized by those who are giving due attention to their business. Yes, such visits are often important to friendships and business. However, the industrious tradesman should avoid visits that involve idle conversation or gossip, or discussions that tend to judge or condemn others who by their absence are unable to defend themselves, or talk that criticizes public officials on matters one really knows little about. Instead, his visits should usually be kept short, serious and cheerful. In that way, he may leave a bit of goodness wherever he goes and a desire in his friends to see him again.

Lastly, diligence can help reduce what might be called "unseasonable devotion." By this I do not mean to discourage religious worship since businesses are generally, in this respect, already cold enough. But some people have in them a careless form of enthusiasm in religious matters, which causes them to neglect their responsibilities to family and friends. Their families and work suffer because of this. Work is left undone at home, and other obligations are not met, while they seem to run from sermon to sermon. Such behavior can't be justified. Still, all industrious tradesmen should be able to redeem some time from their work for public or private devotion. Such time will help improve and delight the mind, as well as refresh the body. However, he should be careful to do this in a way that is consistent with the following:

1. *It should not become stressful mentally.*

2. *It should be consistent with his lawful calling so that God is truly served.*

3. *It should provide sufficient time for reflection and practice*, for the great end of devotion is to help us arrive with safety and joy at a better state. "Teaching us that, denying ungodliness and worldly lusts, we should live soberly, righteously, and godly, in this present world." (Titus 2:12).

THE MOTIVATION OF DILIGENCE

Let the religious tradesman be motivated to be industrious, thereby contributing, with the favor of providence, to our temporal prosperity. Experience reveals to us that we find more inward peace and satisfaction when we diligently pursue our callings than when we waste our time on foolish matters. It increases our appreciation of the rest and refreshments in life, for food as well as, "The sleep of a labouring man is sweet, whether he eat little or much: but the abundance of the rich will not suffer him to sleep." (Ecclesiastes 5:12). Still, let us be very cautious that our diligent behavior does not turn into greed and thereby lose its benefit as a virtue, and become a curse instead of a blessing.

THE BLESSINGS OF DILIGENCE

Let the blessed God be owned and honored, by humble prayer, to bless your diligence, and be given affectionate praise and gratitude for any success you may have. "But thou shalt remember the LORD thy God: for it is he that giveth thee power to get wealth, that he may establish his covenant which he sware unto thy fathers, as it is this day" (Deuteronomy 8:18). In the Psalms, we read that "It is vain for you to rise up early, to sit up late, to eat the bread of sorrows: for so he giveth his beloved sleep." (Psalm 127:2). God governs and influences the minds of others, and directs all those circumstances that must work together for you to be successful. His blessings are preserved by His providence, or otherwise a thousand accidents would deprive us of them.

Spirituality and Diligence

Let us close this chapter with an obvious reflection. Is diligence a duty in the common business of this life? If so, how much more is it in the great concerns of religion and an eternal world? If we don't receive temporal blessings without labor and care, how much less will we develop habits of virtue and goodness, and the rewards of glory and happiness, without diligence?

God will not carry us to heaven like stones, without any sense or motion of our own. Instead, He requires us to respect His eternal grace and favor by striving for it before He gives it to us. Since laziness is an obvious cause of many who are now living in poverty, so it will be the cause of their future misery. They will not be seeking after their salvation, even though such spiritual labor is accompanied with real pleasure and sweetness. Shake off this contemptible disease of the soul! Don't be concerned with insignificant matters, denounce any cold or dreary attitudes you might have, and pursue heavenly and true riches instead. Let what's been said here be a guide for the prosperity of your souls, as well as that of your callings.

Summary

The following list provides a summary of what's been discussed:

1. *Be serious about utilizing everything in the service and love of the ever-blessed God.*

2. *Use your time wisely.* Don't misuse it or waste it, while leaving important work undone.

3. *Lay hold of every opportunity for doing or receiving good.*

4. *Pay appropriate attention to the more minor things,* although nothing that relates to God is ever minor. So don't completely ignore the smaller matters, and let no sin be allowed. "For a man may as surely bleed to death by the wound of a small knife, as by that of a sword."

5. *Reject that which distracts you from important spiritual matters.* Let not the world, the flesh, or the devil, draw your minds away from the love and duty that you owe to God, and those matters which are necessary to the salvation of the soul. Be careful that you do not seek to substitute your own effort for the grace and righteousness of the Lord Jesus Christ. Such effort on your part would be utterly lost and fruitless, since it is by His perfect merits (rested in by faith) and not your good works that will justify you before God. It is in His grace and strength, and not your vigilance and care, that must enable you to fulfill the duties of the Christian life.

SCRIPTURE REFERENCES FOR CHAPTER 4

"And Pharaoh spake unto Joseph, saying, Thy father and thy brethren are come unto thee: The land of Egypt is before thee; in the best of the land make thy father and brethren to dwell; in the land of Goshen let them dwell: and if thou knowest any men of activity among them, then make them rulers over my cattle." (Genesis 47:5-6).

"And the man Jeroboam was a mighty man of valour: and Solomon seeing the young man that he was industrious, he made him ruler over all the charge of the house of Joseph." (1 Kings 11:28).

OF DILIGENCE

"He becometh poor that dealeth with a slack hand: but the hand of the diligent maketh rich. He that gathereth in summer is a wise son: but he that sleepeth in harvest is a son that causeth shame." (Proverbs 10:4-5).

"He that tilleth his land shall be satisfied with bread: but he that followeth vain persons is void of understanding. The hand of the diligent shall bear rule: but the slothful shall be under tribute. The slothful man roasteth not that which he took in hunting: but the substance of a diligent man is precious." (Proverbs 12:11,24,27).

"He also that is slothful in his work is brother to him that is a great waster." (Proverbs 18:9).

"The sluggard will not plow by reason of the cold; therefore shall he beg in harvest, and have nothing. Love not sleep, lest thou come to poverty; open thine eyes, and thou shalt be satisfied with bread." (Proverbs 20:4,13).

"He that loveth pleasure shall be a poor man: he that loveth wine and oil shall not be rich." (Proverbs 21:17).

"Seest thou a man diligent in his business? he shall stand before kings; he shall not stand before mean men." (Proverbs 22:29).

"I went by the field of the slothful, and by the vineyard of the man void of understanding. So shall thy poverty come as one that travelleth; and thy want as an armed man." (Proverbs 24:30,34).

"Yet a little sleep, a little slumber, a little folding of the hands to sleep: So shall thy poverty come as one that travelleth, and thy want as an armed man." (Proverbs 6:10-11).

"Whatsoever thy hand findeth to do, do it with thy might; for there is no work, nor device, nor knowledge, nor wisdom, in the grave, whither thou goest." (Ecclesiastes 9:10).

CHAPTER FIVE
Of Justice

> *The just man walketh in his integrity:*
> *his children are blessed after him.*
> PROVERBS 20:7

JUSTICE, AS IT RELATES TO HOW MEN DEAL WITH ONE ANOTHER, is expressed in that divine rule of our blessed Lord: "Therefore all things whatsoever ye would that men should do to you, do ye even so to them: for this is the law and the prophets." (Matthew 7:12). Hence, in all cases, do to others what you would have them do to you in similar circumstances. This habit of mind, as with diligence, is a virtue that is the same for the true Christian as for others. However, for believers, it is founded upon our faith in the Lord Jesus, reverence to God, and a love of goodness. I characterize it as a habit of mind because it refers not only to how we act but also to the general tone of our lives.

A man may appear pale out of fear or red from blushing. But since these were not characteristics of his complexion, we wouldn't call him a pale or ruddy man. They were merely secondary and momentary, "Lord, who shall abide in thy tabernacle? who shall dwell in thy holy hill? He that walketh uprightly, and worketh righteousness, and speaketh the truth in his heart. He that backbiteth not with his tongue, nor doeth evil to his neighbour, nor taketh up a reproach against his neighbour. In whose eyes a vile person is contemned; but he honoureth them that fear the LORD. He that sweareth to his own hurt, and changeth not. He that putteth not out his money to usury, nor taketh reward against the innocent. He that doeth these things shall never be moved." (Psalm 15).

OUR OBLIGATIONS TO JUSTICE

First, we will describe several obligations we have regarding justice.

1. *It is part of the light of both nature and reason.* Men are not like the fish of the sea, made to prey and devour one another. Instead, all men deserve justice. Therefore, it is reasonable that all man treat one another in ways that help to bring justice. The consciences of men reveal this principle so clearly that it is impossible for it to be eliminated somehow, even though there are some who act harshly against it. The Roman emperor, Severus, so greatly admired the golden rule of our Savior, "And as ye would that men should do to you, do ye also to them likewise," (Luke 6:31) that he made it his motto and instructed that it be written on his doors and buildings, and added the divine Author to his list of gods. Would that God inscribe it, not so much on walls, as in the hearts and lives of those who call themselves Christians.

2. *We are required to practice justice because of the moral law of God, which is summarized in the Ten Commandments.* For example, "Thou shalt not covet thy neighbour's house, thou shalt not covet thy neighbour's wife, nor his manservant, nor his maidservant, nor his ox, nor his ass, nor any thing that is thy neighbour's" (Exodus 20:17) refers to certain principles while "Thou shalt not steal" (Exodus 20:15) refers to certain practices. They all deal with justice and are further expressed by various

OF JUSTICE

commands. God has said, "Keep ye judgment, and do justice: for my salvation is near to come, and my righteousness to be revealed." (Isaiah 56:1). We are also commanded the following: "Thou shalt not defraud thy neighbour, neither rob him: the wages of him that is hired shall not abide with thee all night until the morning." (Leviticus 19:13). In Deuteronomy we correspondingly read, "That which is altogether just shalt thou follow, that thou mayest live, and inherit the land which the LORD thy God giveth thee." (Deuteronomy 16:20).

God has strengthened these precepts with certain threats of severe punishment for disobedience. We can see many visible instances of such punishment in the world, but many more are reserved to the great and solemn Day of Judgment. The gospel of Christ binds the consciences of all who expect to receive a share of His blessings to this matter of justice: "Teaching us that, denying ungodliness and worldly lusts, we should live soberly, righteously, and godly, in this present world." (Titus 2:12). Not only that, it serves to deprive the unjust from the benefit of the blessings, for "If therefore ye have not been faithful in the unrighteous mammon, who will commit to your trust the true riches?" (Luke 16:11). That is, such are utterly excluded from both the hope of future glory and its rewards.

We are told in 1st Corinthians: "Know ye not that the unrighteous shall not inherit the kingdom of God? Be not deceived: neither fornicators, nor idolaters, nor adulterers, nor effeminate, nor abusers of themselves with mankind," (1 Corinthians 6:9). Therefore, those who allow themselves to violate the laws of justice do damage to the Christian witness, In such cases, whatever one's profession of faith may be, it is either insincere or false. A man who is unjust toward others is not true before God, nor can he be accepted of Him.

So, not only are we obliged to honor justice because of duty and conscience, but also because it can be beneficial to our business. It will naturally tend to help our business since it reveals good character, upon which much of the tradesman's success depends. Everyone prefers to deal with a man who has a reputation of honesty and justice. And, although some men may be afflicted because of their indiscretions or divine providence, God blesses many others as a demonstration of his love to righteousness and the goodness of His providence in this world. "A faithful man shall abound with blessings: but he that maketh haste to be rich shall not be innocent." (Proverbs 28:20).

Shame and misery are the natural fruits of injustice and fraud. When men have increased their wealth from the spoils of others, divine vengeance often consumes them. So detestable is this sin to God that even their descendents shall feel the effects of His anger against it. We may often observe how ill-gotten wealth is wasted in the hands of those for whom it was unjustly acquired.

THE APPLICATION OF JUSTICE

Now that we've considered the nature of justice and our obligation to practice it, let's look at several examples in which the tradesman should apply it.

DECISION MAKING

Justice compels the tradesman to make wise business decisions. He should see that he neither sells too high nor buys too cheap. That is, he deals with others as he would have others deal with him. Let's look at what this means.

1. *Doing this requires us to price what we trade in a way that provides for a reasonable, not excessive, gain.* There is no specific rule as to what this gain should be for all tradesmen. It is not always based on what the commodity cost us. For example, what if, because of our own ignorance, we paid a price that was very high. Should others have to pay for our ignorance? On the other hand, what if in some special situation we were able to buy something for relatively very little. Are we then obligated to sell it for very little? The rates at which others sell the same things cannot always be the proper measure of gain. They may be required to sell under a certain rate for some reason. Why should their situation influence what I charge? Perhaps they are seeking to undersell others with regard to certain items simply to gain customers, while overpricing other items. Why should their poor business practices control how legitimate tradesmen do business? What if others set prices that are unreasonable and extravagant. Why must I be governed by their greed?

What something used to sell for is not a sufficient measure of value today. Everyone knows that prices will vary, and what was worth so much last year may not be worth half as much this year. What is necessary to maintain the tradesman and his family is not a sure guide either. The needs of some families are more than the needs of others; for example, there may be much illness in one family. Some say we should charge as much as we can get for an item. However, this is not a just measure of what our profit should be. For example, we might be able sell a particular item for twice its value to an unskillful or unwary customer, which is downright injustice and fraud. Finally, what we think is the inherent value of something cannot always be our rule for pricing. The reason is for some things simply have unknown components of value.

Therefore, the surest rule that we can use is the market price. It is general and therefore the most reliable. It is also the least influenced by a few individuals. A reasonable allowance is given for a person's time, labor, difficulties and skill. There may be certain cases where the tradesman will be justified in raising the price of his goods for certain customers and situations. However, in all cases, he should deal with honesty and justice. He should generally desire to get no more profit from what he sells than that which he would expect to give others for what he buys, remembering "light gains make a heavy purse, but large gains often make a heavy conscience."

2. *Justice forbids us from setting prices that take advantage of those who are needy.* You should be sure not to be the cause of the cries of the poor to God. For example, you shouldn't try to set prices for the labor or goods of others so low that it is impossible for them to live on their profits. Similarly, should they be in a position of having to sell their goods quickly, don't be tempted to withhold from them a reasonable gain. I heard of one disgusting tradesman who bought manufactured metal from a needy workman at the same price for which un-manufactured metal was selling, and then glory in his bargain. However common or profitable such practices might be, they are unjust and oppressive. If there is any providence of God in this world, or any truth in His Word, surely such wicked behavior will receive His curse.

If you're ever tempted by greed to do such things, consider what God has said, "What mean ye that ye beat my people to pieces, and grind the faces of the poor? saith the Lord GOD of hosts." (Isaiah 3:15). And, if you've been guilty of such sin, then to prevent shame and misunderstanding, sincerely repent and commit yourself to more humane and Christian methods of trading in the future. Don't let the circumstances of others encourage you to take advantage of their great need. And, if your fellow tradesman should need a commodity to supply his customer, show your generosity and honor by treating him as you would want him to treat you. In no case should you be seeking opportunities to take advantage of others, for you would not want to be exploited in this way. Instead, you should treat those who come to you in need with greater honesty and compassion than those who are not so disadvantaged.

3. We should not take advantage of the others with less business skill. We are not all endowed with the same abilities and knowledge in business. Some may tend to be more forgetful and make more mistakes than others. But first we must recognize that no one, including ourselves, can perfectly judge the value or goodness of every commodity they might want to buy or sell. Therefore, if it's not just that others take advantage of our ignorance or mistakes, it is equally not just for us to do the same to others. What is not right in one case is certainly not right in the other. There is no excuse for such practices. Therefore, you should not try to defend them. Instead, remember that the just and righteous God never gives anyone superior understanding or skills so that they should be used for selfish purposes. Also, just because others might deal with you wrongly, you are not to deal with them the same way. The criminal conduct of others can never excuse your behavior. In fact, the more widespread a certain wrong practice is, the more honor and virtue there is in not conforming to it. "That no man go beyond and defraud his brother in any matter: because that the Lord is the avenger of all such, as we also have forewarned you and testified." (1 Thessalonians 4:6).

4. Don't make deals with those who have no legitimate stake in a particular agreement. For example, in the case of selling goods, be careful not to become involved with those who may not be trusted with money. Another example, when buying, is to avoid making deals where you either know, or greatly suspect, the goods to be stolen. Yes, such situations may offer opportunity for large profits, but the issue of your guilt is more important. Those who assist or encourage others in their wickedness should dwell on that Divine censure: "When thou sawest a thief, then thou consentedst with him, and hast been partaker with adulterers." (Psalm 50:18).

He that knowingly conspires or assists in evil activity shares in the guilt of it. Even if you are able to escape the laws of man that strictly forbid such things, the penetrating eye of God always see what you do. Sooner or later, He will make known to you His resentment regarding your stealing and greed. Don't try to claim that it's a matter of your right to do business, for what honest man will buy a stolen horse on the market if he knows or suspects it is stolen?

And don't try to argue that, if you don't buy such goods, someone else will. Know that the wickedness of others gives you no excuse to sin. Its odd that men, who usually act with reason and good sense, are so ready to violate their conscience when presented with an opportunity for a quick and easy profit. It is better that you be poor and keep your integrity than to get involved in dishonest business deals.

5. *Use honesty and openness in your business dealings.* Buyers are supposed to be watching for common and noticeable faults in a product. However, if there is something wrong with the product you're selling that is hidden or hard to detect, something which otherwise might cause a buyer not to purchase from you or to reduce the price he is willing to pay, then you should sell at a price that takes the defects into account. The faults might be such that the buyer would not want the product at all if he knew about them, regardless of what you, as the seller, might think about them. I fear that such honesty does not always occur.

On the other side of the deal, we consider the buyer who, when informed of the defects of a product, uses them to bargain for a lower price although he really doesn't think the defects sufficient to justify the price he offers. He is equally guilty with the seller who claims his goods faultless when he knows otherwise. Ask your conscience whether such conduct can be justified before God, or whether it represents doing unto others as you would have done unto you. If you say that it is a necessary part of doing business to buy damaged and faulty goods along with others and that you must sell them, I say that you should try to buy as few of them as possible, and sell to those who know about the defects. Divine providence can reward those who deny themselves personal profits via the ignorance of others.

FINANCIAL RESPONSIBILITIES

Justice requires that regular payment of all just debts be on time. We must be very cautious about becoming financially indebted to anyone, especially unbelievers. For example, the Word of God advises against becoming unequally yoked with unbelievers. However, in cases where debt exists, one should make payments as they've been agreed to. If possible, he should seek to eliminate them altogether. But, when they exist, he should make every effort possible to make payment as scheduled. Perhaps the most inexcusable violation of justice is the tradesman who attempts to defraud creditors by changing the terms of their agreement in a way to enrich himself. How many sins man is willing to commit for a little monetary gain! He sometimes lies, steals or conceals, showing contempt for God's law and justice and injuring others. How can one hope to escape the righteous judgment of God when guilty of such crimes?

WEIGHTS AND MEASURES

Justice includes that we use exact "weights and measures." Without these, commerce can become corrupted. A buyer may walk away from a deal satisfied, thinking that he had received the quantity he bargained for, when he had not. Nothing can be more contrary to integrity and justice than such cheating. For example, we are told in Deuteronomy: "Thou shalt not have in thy bag divers weights, a great and a small. Thou shalt not have in thine house divers measures, a great and a small. But thou shalt have a perfect and just weight, a perfect and just measure shalt thou have: that thy days may be lengthened in the land which the LORD thy God giveth thee." (Deuteronomy 25:13-15). Comparably, Micah the prophet writes, "Are there yet the treasures of wickedness in the house of the wicked, and the scant measure that is abominable? Shall I count them pure with the wicked balances, and with the bag of deceitful weights?" (Micah 6:10-11). Clearly, God detests weights and measures that are not "perfect and just." We should all avoid them. Buyers and sellers alike should not seek to obtain more than what he agrees to, or by any deceitful technique to interfere with just business dealings.

Fraud associated with the value of products or goods is found in other areas than weights and measures. One example is the tradesman who arranges the lighting in his shop in such a way as to intentionally misrepresent his products as better than they really are. Then, when the buyer gets home and takes a closer look at what he has bought, he finds it to be something different. An injustice has occurred, one which is basically the same thing as deceiving one's neighbor. Indeed, it is like picking the pocket of the buyer for an amount above the real worth of the product.

PRODUCT QUALITY

Justice requires that the products a tradesman provides not be defective. In some places, laws may require that certain goods or products meet various quality standards. However, since cases of fraud can occur in so many different ways, it is impossible to

OF JUSTICE

catch them all; and, unless men are convicted of God and conscience, they will find a way around the laws.

Justice serves to teach the tradesman to do such work for others as he would have done for himself. Therefore, all products that he sells should be of reasonable quality and require reasonable maintenance or care. It's true that, due to its materials, price or design, not every product will require the same amount of labor or care. However, justice requires that every product have at least the level of quality that is common or expected for such goods in the marketplace. A violation would be the use of lower quality materials even though the final product met the needs of the customer, at least to his knowledge, even though, because of his ignorance, he paid a price higher than the true value of the commodity. Don't try to claim that market prices are not sufficient to provide quality products, for the reason why prices are reduced on a product is usually due to its lower quality. We often discover that, when quality goes up, prices will go up. We also find that those who do the best work also tend to make the most profit.

TAXES AND FEES

Justice requires the tradesman to be ready and willing to pay all the fees, taxes or customs required by law. Since the tradesman enjoys the benefits and protection of government, he should be willing to financially support it as required. Justice requires that you promptly deal with any such obligations that you don't find appropriate. However, if the civil government has already determined them lawful for the benefit and protection of the people, then you are obligated. It is not sufficient to argue that, because the government already has enough money, they wouldn't miss your contribution. Fraud is not an acceptable response to legitimate financial obligations imposed by the government, any more than a tenant regarding the fees required by his landlord.

It may be true that there seems to be no end to taxation, or that security is not being adequately provided, and so forth. However, it is hard to prove such accusations. One cannot always put the blame of certain lower-level government workers on the chief magistrates, unless there is significant evidence of neglect over time. It may be that certain government employees, seeking personal rather public good, are so negligent that they need to be corrected by those in authority over them.

Neither is it enough for you to simply agree to suffer the penalty for withholding lawful financial taxes should you be discovered. Even common thieves might make that plea if it benefits them. Lawful penalties are made to restrain evil, those whose conscience towards God or sense of justice to man does not motivate them to do what's right. It would harm your reputation to be associated with such behavior.

If you expect blessings from Heaven, don't withhold from the civil authorities what they require by law. Since God has ordained them, they have a legitimate claim to financial support. This is a matter of justice. "Then saith he unto them, Render therefore unto Caesar the things which are Caesar's; and unto God the things that are God's." (Matthew 22:21).

LEGAL OBLIGATIONS

Justice requires the tradesman to respect the laws of the society in which he lives. This assumes, however, the laws do not require you to disobey God's laws. On the other hand, justice and conscience compel us to follow the laws imposed on us by the civil government even when they may interfere with our private interests. For example, if you find that you have interfered with some law related to your business, you should either adhere to it or cheerfully submit to any fines imposed on you. Say you're prohibited from importing or exporting a particularly profitable product or commodity because it might harm those who are poor

OF JUSTICE

or perhaps help those who are public enemies. Justice requires that you comply with such restrictions. Perhaps there is a law against your hiring foreign workers in your business, so that those who have served you as a regular apprentice might not be kept from employment. Justice and loyalty should convince you to obey such a law. In summary, being faithful and true to our obligations requires that we should always consider what is most beneficial to society as well as to ourselves, the future as well as the present.

FAIR TREATMENT

Justice demands that you treat fellow tradesmen fairly. Although every man may use all lawful methods to increase and secure what he has, this does not include doing that which hinders those poorer than ourselves. In addition, justice forbids us from taking customers or business associates away from others in ways that are less than honorable. You should never be involved with making unjust allegations or derogatory suggestions regarding the goods or character of your fellow tradesman, seeking to increase your business at the expense of his. Let it always be your governing principle to do unto others as you would have them do unto you.

Masters should be content to lose some of their customers when an apprentice leaves them to set up his own shop (this being understood from the beginning). However, apprentices should be careful not to try to gain customers in any unworthy way, or to do anything other than that which is typical and has been agreed to. He should remember that, should he someday have apprentices, there may come a time when he will face the same circumstances from a different perspective.

Again, it is contrary to the laws of justice and charity to be trading products in a way that deprives many to enrich a few, whether it be the work of societies or individuals. We are commanded to love our neighbors as ourselves, and not to seek to benefit ourselves by acting unfairly toward others. It is reasonable that men benefit from their own labor and business activities. Those who deprive them of this by their own greed or self-enrichment schemes make themselves public enemies. Men may "boast when they do well for themselves; and others may bless the covetous whom God abhors." But our common and loving Father cannot but hate situations where gains are obtained by oppression, and punish those who use such get-rich-quick methods. We often see the effects of this in the fall and ruin of those who sought to enrich themselves by unrighteous behavior.

It is also inconsistent with justice and fairness for the larger or more successful tradesman or craftsman to try to undersell other smaller businessmen at prices that preclude them from maintaining their customers or surviving on their profits. Such conduct is particularly criminal when its intent is to weaken and bankrupt others.

Lastly, I will mention that you should not tolerate unjust transactions between you and your partners in trade, to whom you are bound by law, conscience and mutual confidence. For partners to undermine or rob one another is a crime that deserves severe condemnation. Only those who have lost all love of virtue or fear of shame can practice such activities.

OBLIGATIONS TO EMPLOYEES

Justice requires the tradesman to truly care for his apprentices. It is prudent to choose apprentices with good character and temper, and abilities suitable for the business, and to avoid those who simply need some quick income or business, the impact of which could be years. Those you find worthy should be accepted like a member of your family. Accordingly, justice requires that you treat them in the same way you would treat one of your own children.

OF JUSTICE

Beware of treating helpers harshly or with undue severity. To do that would discourage them in their work for you, in addition to making their time and life a burden. Perhaps you were once in the same situation they're in now; so try to avoid inflicting upon them what you may have justly deemed a hardship when you were an apprentice. Remember that you also have a Master in heaven who rules by love and just authority, not by severity and vengeance. So you should seek to imitate Him in that way.

You should manage your employees in such a way as to command their love and esteem as well as their respect and obedience toward you. Work to maintain your authority over them by leading a life of virtue and religion. When you do this, you gain admiration and respect more effectively than by any severe gravity in your words and behavior. Be careful not to overburden workers or to encourage their bitterness, lest they cry unto God against you. Don't forget their young age, and bear with their shortcomings or weaknesses. Be sure not to find fault in them without cause, or to refuse their apologies. Keep in mind Job's reflection in a similar situation: "If I did despise the cause of my manservant or of my maidservant, when they contended with me; What then shall I do when God riseth up? and when he visiteth, what shall I answer him?" (Job 31:13-14). So, give them opportunities to rest and refresh themselves during the workday, for their health and comfort. Be as ready to commend them when they do well as when they don't. This helps establish good will between you and your employees, remembering that "Thou shalt not curse the deaf, nor put a stumblingblock before the blind, but shalt fear thy God" (Leviticus 19:14).

On the other hand, you shouldn't be pampering your helpers either. Maintain your authority over them in a way that contributes to an attitude of respect for God and each other. You should never tolerate sinful behavior. Provide an example and policy that is fair and truthful, before God and man. Most of all, be certain to safeguard them from any association with evil company. To do this, find out from them how they spend their free time. Encourage them in the Faith, that they spend time with God. Many people trace problems in their spiritual journey to their indulgence in false notions of liberty. I am unable to understand how certain tradesmen plan to give an account to God and their consciences regarding their neglect toward their employees. I don't think anything has contributed more to the corruption of the upcoming generation.

How justly may God reprimand the selfishness and hypocrisy of those who require strict obedience to their own commands while neglecting God's. Therefore, be attentive to the lives of your employees, noticing who their friends are and listening to them. Your obvious efforts at helping them avoid inappropriate or wasteful activities may bother them for now but, later on, after their reflection, they will come to bless you, and bless God for your caring for them. Finally, when you ask your employees to travel as part of business, be alert to those who may not have sufficient wisdom or virtue to protect themselves from the numerous temptations out in the world, and by which many young people have been destroyed.

FAMILY RESPONSIBILITIES

Justice should motivate the tradesman to make due provisions for his wife and children, should he have them. Wives deserve substantial consideration. As your helpmeet, she works either in the shop or in the family to add to your estate, and to manage the affairs of the household. She has left her family and friends to join with you, casting herself upon your love and care. You're therefore obligated to provide for her as best as you can.

Your children are also an important part of your life. And, since they came into the world dependent upon you, it would be

OF JUSTICE

both unnatural and unjust for you not to provide for their needs. Yet, sadly, many tradesmen, through their laziness and negligence, bring misery and suffering to their distressed families. They lose their business. The wife is forced to live on help from her friends, or languish in poverty. The children wander poor and forsaken. O wretched injustice! Can the posterity of such men rise up and call them blessed, who make them heirs of nothing but poverty and distress? Or will those who are cruel to their own families seek to excuse themselves because they have, at one time, acted fairly toward others?

Limit what you spend on clothes, food and furniture. Avoid unreasonable or expensive luxuries. Be attentive to your work and its concerns, so that your family will not need to rely on the charity of friends. If possible, put aside some money to care for them should you not be able to provide. Don't be like those who are not concerned for their offspring after you're gone. "A good man leaveth an inheritance to his children's children: and the wealth of the sinner is laid up for the just." (Proverbs 13:22). The Psalmist reflects similarly, "Wealth and riches shall be in his house: and his righteousness endureth for ever." (Psalm 112:3).

CHARITY

It is just that the tradesmen shows mercy toward the poor, for righteousness includes charity. Men are only stewards of what is given them by God, Who is the original Proprietor of all things. He allows us to use what is appropriate for our needs, and appoints the poor and needy to receive the rest. We are not therefore to withhold good from them to whom it is due when it is within our power to do so. We should seek to use what we have as good servants of our great Master. Therefore, we should regulate our expenses and assist others when possible, so that with our hands and heads we will do the thing which is good, "...that he may have to give to him that needeth." (Ephesians 4:28). The goodness of God is His glory. What better attitude among His creatures, or what greater delight to a humane and pious heart, or what more generous reward from a good God is there than a sincere desire to imitate His goodness? May the tradesmen be careful to trust God with future events, and to extend the compassion within his heart to that which is appropriate.

There is a lot of opportunity to serve the poor and needy. Perhaps you have some relatives that are needy, or you know of some poor among God's children. Maybe you know of a poor, faithful minister of Christ who could use your help, or a brilliant but somewhat impoverished scholar who might become an instrument of public good with your aid. One might have heard of some group of people somewhere in special need of missionaries or Bibles. Maybe you've recently read about some young men who need assistance in developing or finding a trade, or others who have the skills but not the tools or initial supply of goods. Think of the poor tradesmen or housekeepers who are often looking for work, who may be part of a large family hit by severe hardships.

Some of these individuals, whose patience prevents them from complaining about their situation or whose shyness keeps them from asking for work, will fall into misery from their sufferings. Do not forget the virtuous maiden who, with a little financial assistance, might be enabled to find temporary employment until she is able to find a suitable marriage partner but, being poor and neglected, is exposed to many temptations. There are schools for neglected children, relief groups for the sick or lame, and organizations that assist the aged and helpless, all of which are appropriate for your charity according to your ability to help.

So that you may be charitable toward others, consider regularly putting some money aside for this purpose, as God has blessed you and according to your income. In this way, you can better serve the uncertainties of others, who may only occasionally stretch out their hands in need of help. I believe you'll find that building such a resource for charitable giving will thrive, because of its worthiness through the faithfulness and bounty of God.

RESTORATION AND RESTITUTION

Finally, justice demands a quick resolution to anything that may have been unlawfully obtained. This is so obvious, that one would think little needs to be said to prove the point. Nevertheless, I'll provide a couple of examples just to be clear.

1. ***Man's conscience can never be pacified nor his guilt removed as long as he holds onto ill-gotten gains.*** No repentance is sincere that does not include the restoration of that which was unjustly obtained. Indeed, repentance must include undoing, as far as possible, that which had been wrongly done. If it was criminal for you to injure your neighbor at the start, the crime remains as long as you continue to withhold from him that which he is due.

Scripture tells us that when we trespass against others, such as by defrauding them, God deems such injustice to be against Himself. It is a violation of His law and shows contempt for His authority. The Bible tells us that, "Then they shall confess their sin which they have done: and he shall recompense his trespass with the principal thereof, and add unto it the fifth part thereof, and give it unto him against whom he hath trespassed." (Numbers 5:7). The consciences of all men are bound to this moral justice until the end of time.

When Nehemiah addressed the Jews, who had been guilty of oppression, he promised that they would have to restore that which they had wrongly possessed. To this he added from the Lord: "Also I shook my lap, and said, So God shake out every man from his house, and from his labour, that performeth not this promise, even thus be he shaken out, and emptied. And all the congregation said, Amen, and praised the LORD. And the people did according to this promise." (Nehemiah 5:13). Zacchaeus immediately fell under the conviction of this command when our blessed Savior invited Himself to his house. He knew of no better way to express his conviction of his past errors than to say: "...Behold, Lord, the half of my goods I give to the poor; and if I have taken any thing from any man by false accusation, I restore him fourfold." (Luke 19:8). This shows us that the consciences of all men know that restitution is just and, that the man who becomes saved after injuring his neighbor will seek to make restitution.

2. Justice is in your interest. God, as Governor of righteousness, will ensure that wealth that comes from injustice will never be a blessing to them. Often, God will blow such gains away, like chaff before wind. Even, when He does not do so, the Divine curse will remain and, like leprosy, it will infect everything you have. Who would forfeit their wealth gained honestly, for the sake of holding on to a little obtained unjustly? It would be better to take any ill-gotten goods and cast them into the sea than to have them destroy you. Likewise you should esteem it a thousand times higher to live poor and just, and then to die blessed, rather than live and die with a curse.

If you are unable to make full restitution but have the will to do so, you surely ought still to mourn over the fact that you have injured others. You should accept God's justice on the matter over the near term and be ready to make some degree of restitution whenever you become able. If you seek to avoid making restitution because you fear the shame or loss of reputation, perhaps you might consider asking a faithful friend to help you make things right without being identified. To sin is shame. However, you should try to move beyond it by seeking to somehow restore righteousness and justice. After all, what shame can there be in doing that which is good?

Still, if it is your foolish embarrassment or greed that stands in the way of your making restitution, remember that there will come a day when your injustices will be brought before God, angels and men. What unspeakable shame and confusion will then cover your face when it is revealed that, after all the reproof of reason and conscience, you chose to live and die in those sins? If you claim that the persons you injured are no longer alive and you don't know whom to make restitution to, I say their heirs or executors may have a rightful claim to it. And, if they cannot be located after much effort, Scripture tells us who should be compensated: "But if the man have no kinsman to recompense the trespass unto, let the trespass be recompensed unto the LORD, even to the priest; beside the ram of the atonement, whereby an atonement shall be made for him." (Numbers 5:8). God's church and the poor are His recipients of all estates forfeited to His honor and government. When we give to the poor, it is like lending to the Lord, when we do it out of compassion. Similarly, when we give to God, He declares it an act of justice.

Conclusion

In conclusion, let's review some of the most important matters of justice.

1. *Reflect on your past conduct with regard to the important responsibility of justice.* Perhaps you have so secretively taken care of certain injustices that your reputation has not been harmed. But what about your conscience? Do you not remember that questionable deal you made, where the products were purchased by deceit and lies? The time you biased the tools you use for weighing and measuring goods. What does your conscience say about such things? See if there are not cases where you have been guilty. Deal with the matter now, realizing that the longer you wait, the worse it will get. Don't shut your eyes to the truth or try to find an excuse that will not stand the test of the Judgment day. " ... break off thy sins by righteousness, and thine iniquities by shewing mercy ... " (Daniel 4:27). Seek Divine forgiveness through a sincere repentance before God and a humble faith in Christ Jesus the Lord while forgiveness may be had.

2. Let all that you do be according to the rules of justice. Consider nothing truly gained unless you gained it honestly. When in doubt, always take the surer path, and do that which appears to be the most honorable, just and charitable. Don't seek to live on the edge of lawlessness, for he who always walks as close to the river's bank as possible is in danger of falling in. In matters of duty, it's usually best to do the most you can. However, because of our tendency to be selfish, in situations where you have an advantage, be careful not to abuse it. Show favor to the poor, initiative to the unskillful, and moderation and fairness to all. Resolve, by the grace of God, that although you may not be very rich, you will always be very just. This is the path to both a good conscience and sufficient estate. Whatever you acquire through diligent work and God's blessing, you can enjoy now and leave to comfort your family down the road.

To this end:

Let the fear of God rule in your heart. Fear of shame may restrain some men from unjust behavior, but nothing less than a true fear of God will make them fully just and honest.

Conquer any love for the world that you might have. A greedy and selfish temper is the source of much injustice and oppression. Men would never expose themselves to the wrath of God, injure their neighbors, or jeopardize their reputation for a little financial gain if their love for the world was not excessive.

Learn to be content with what God has given you in this life and trust Him for the future. God's providence oversees and directs all of the situations of His creatures. He knows both our needs and what would harm us. Thus, He will be sure to bring the most good to those who trust in Him. However, some men seek to live independently from God. Others, after neglecting and disobeying Him, then come to believe that God does not care about them or become unwilling to place themselves at His mercy. And, although justice and fairness may sometimes interfere with the financial success of the faithful Christian, he should be confident that God will provide both his temporal and spiritual needs. He is too great and too good to permit his obedient servants to be denied their needs.

Love your neighbor as yourself. Put yourself in his place when you deal with him. This will help you avoid doing that which would dishonor him or be unfair.

Finally, since this and every other virtue comes from Christ Jesus, the Fountain of all wisdom and grace, practice it by maintaining a true and living faith in Him, as the great Mediator. If you do this, whatever rewards you might receive in this world, you will not fail to be abundantly rewarded in the next world, in the presence and favor of the just and righteous God. Still, let no man be so vain as to think that the Christian faith will benefit the one who denies its precepts, or that the righteousness of Christ was meant to justify or save the unrepentant and unrighteous dealer.

3. *As much as possible, encourage others to live justly.* Be sure to teach and instill principles of justice and honesty in your children. Don't permit anything less. In your words and your life, stand fast against any kind of deceitful or harmful dealings with others. Don't tolerate or become a part of such behavior, in many cases, the one who doesn't try to obstruct an injustice becomes part of it. In the groups that you interface with, seek to influence or reform them in this matter as you think necessary. In this way, you honor the Gospel, you help stop the work of its enemies, and you establish a good reputation among men. Seek to live in peace and die in comfort (through the grace of the Redeemer), and to leave a blessing wherever you go. Amen.

SCRIPTURE REFERENCES FOR CHAPTER 5

"And take double money in your hand; and the money that was brought again in the mouth of your sacks, carry it again in your hand; peradventure it was an oversight:" (Genesis 43:12).

"Thou shalt not steal. Thou shalt not covet thy neighbour's house, thou shalt not covet thy neighbour's wife, nor his manservant, nor his maidservant, nor his ox, nor his ass, nor any thing that is thy neighbour's." (Exodus 20:15,17).

"Thou shalt not defraud thy neighbour, neither rob him: the wages of him that is hired shall not abide with thee all night until the morning. Ye shall do no unrighteousness in judgment, in meteyard, in weight, or in measure." (Leviticus 19:13,35).

"Thou shalt not have in thy bag divers weights, a great and a small. For all that do such things, and all that do unrighteously, are an abomination unto the LORD thy God." (Deuteronomy 25:13,16).

"He hath swallowed down riches, and he shall vomit them up again: God shall cast them out of his belly. Because he hath oppressed and hath forsaken the poor; because he hath violently taken away an house which he builded not; Surely he shall not feel quietness in his belly, he shall not save of that which he desired. In the fulness of his sufficiency he shall be in straits: every

OF JUSTICE

hand of the wicked shall come upon him. All darkness shall be hid in his secret places: a fire not blown shall consume him; it shall go ill with him that is left in his tabernacle. The heaven shall reveal his iniquity; and the earth shall rise up against him." (Job 20:15,19-20,22,27).

"Treasures of wickedness profit nothing: but righteousness delivereth from death. Blessings are upon the head of the just: but violence covereth the mouth of the wicked." (Proverbs 10:2,6).

"A good man obtaineth favour of the LORD: but a man of wicked devices will he condemn. The wicked are overthrown, and are not: but the house of the righteous shall stand." (Proverbs 12:2,7).

"Better is a little with righteousness than great revenues without right." (Proverbs 16:8).

"The just man walketh in his integrity: his children are blessed after him. Bread of deceit is sweet to a man; but afterwards his mouth shall be filled with gravel. An inheritance may be gotten hastily at the beginning; but the end thereof shall not be blessed." (Proverbs 20:7,17,21).

"It is joy to the just to do judgment: but destruction shall be to the workers of iniquity." (Proverbs 21:15).

"He that by usury and unjust gain increaseth his substance, he shall gather it for him that will pity the poor. A faithful man shall abound with blessings: but he that maketh haste to be rich shall not be innocent." (Proverbs 28:8,20).

"As the partridge sitteth on eggs, and hatcheth them not; so he that getteth riches, and not by right, shall leave them in the midst of his days, and at his end shall be a fool." (Jeremiah 17:11).

"Woe unto him that buildeth his house by unrighteousness, and his chambers by wrong; that useth his neighbour's service without wages, and giveth him not for his work;" (Jeremiah

22:13).

"In thee have they taken gifts to shed blood; thou hast taken usury and increase, and thou hast greedily gained of thy neighbours by extortion, and hast forgotten me, saith the Lord GOD. Can thine heart endure, or can thine hands be strong, in the days that I shall deal with thee? I the LORD have spoken it, and will do it" (Ezekiel 22:12,14).

"Thou hast defiled thy sanctuaries by the multitude of thine iniquities, by the iniquity of thy traffick; therefore will I bring forth a fire from the midst of thee, it shall devour thee, and I will bring thee to ashes upon the earth in the sight of all them that behold thee." (Ezekiel 28:18).

"For the wrath of God is revealed from heaven against all ungodliness and unrighteousness of men, who hold the truth in unrighteousness; Being filled with all unrighteousness, fornication, wickedness, covetousness, maliciousness; full of envy, murder, debate, deceit, malignity; whisperers, Without understanding, covenantbreakers, without natural affection, implacable, unmerciful:" (Romans 1:18,29,31).

"That no man go beyond and defraud his brother in any matter: because that the Lord is the avenger of all such, as we also have forewarned you and testified." (1 Thessalonians 4:6).

CHAPTER SIX

Of Truth

*The lip of truth shall
be established for ever...*
PROVERBS 12:19

WE SHOULD BE SEEKERS AND DOERS OF THE TRUTH. Accordingly, we first need to determine whether what we say or do agrees with what we understand or find to be the truth as revealed in Scripture. What we say or do may line up with our understanding of something but not with reality, in which case we have a false understanding of the truth. This may not necessarily cause a problem. However, once we come to understand the truth about something, we become accountable for that knowledge. I say this because the law that requires us to do what is right also requires us to be seekers of the truth.

On the other hand, if what we say or do doesn't line up with what we believe to be the truth, then we're committing a lie, even if what we do happens to agree with what's right or truthful. In such a case, we would be intentionally misrepresenting what we believe to be right or true. Whatever something is in truth, if we imagine it to be something else, we're only really imagining it to be what it is not. We need to remind ourselves that people can both speak and act a lie, for words are simply a way of expressing our beliefs, which are revealed by what we do. For example, "the man that lives as if he had the estate he knows he has not; or was what indeed he knows he is not, doth as truly lie, as if he was continually expressing it by words, if it be done with a design to injure and deceive others." So, we should recognize that not every mistake we make or every time we say something we're unsure of is a lie; neither is every parable or fable we tell. Rather, a lie occurs when someone deliberately falsifies the truth, usually with the intent to deceive.

ON BEING HONEST

I encourage every tradesman to judge matters as they truly are and, when called to talk about them, not to add or take anything away from the truth. For example, he should not intentionally say something about some product on the market that would falsely undervalue it. Instead, he should "walketh uprightly, and worketh righteousness, and speaketh the truth in his heart." (Psalm 15:2). According to his conscience before God and love of virtue, he is bound by the rules of honesty. Let me describe a few examples for the tradesman.

1. *Justice.* Every one deserves to be dealt with honestly. We all dislike being deceived or lied to. So, we're obligated to treat others as we would want to be treated. By what reasoning can we expect that all men should treat us with sincerity and honesty while our conduct toward them is one of lying or fraud? If you expect the truth from others, why shouldn't you be equally truthful with them?

Civil society exists upon some measure of honesty and truthfulness; otherwise, bonds are broken and confidence is destroyed. How can men deal and trade with one another if each cannot believe the other? Unless one regularly speaks the truth, how can he be believed? If a man lies about something in one particular situation, it may be reasonable to think he will lie

OF TRUTH

again in other situations.

We might further note that truth and justice are so closely related to each other that a man who is just in his dealings will also be one who does not have a habit of lying. We should all be very concerned about anything that is destructive to the public good. One reason we were given the gift of speech was to enable us to express our concerns to one another. Lying and falsehood so directly contradict this purpose that we might think it better to be unable to speak at all than to be a liar.

2. *Faith.* Our Christian faith provides us with our strongest obligations to truth and sincerity. We worship and serve the God of Truth. The revelation we believe in is the Gospel of Truth. In all areas, the precepts of our faith compel us toward the love and practice of truth, and the hatred of lying. So contrary is the practice of falsehood and deceit to the Spirit of Christianity, that it utterly excludes those who practice it from sharing in the blessings of the Gospel or the hope of salvation. Yes, the contradiction between a dishonest man and a true Christian is so clear that it is amazing how any can pretend to be the latter whose conduct reveals them to be the former.

3. *Honor.* Men should be motivated to be truthful in what they say not only because of their religious faith but also because it is honorable. It is of a noble spirit to speak the truth. A man of good conscience will also be a man known for his honesty, and be respected by other honorable men. A man who knows himself to be guilty feels a kind of sting in his conscience, even when no one else knows of his guilt. And, if he's found out, he will be filled with shame and confusion. So, honor pleads for honesty in what one says, truthfulness being the best way to achieve and hold on to your credibility.

Here is a comparison worth remembering. We will tend to

believe a man who is known to be honest, even regarding doubtful things. On the other hand, a man who has a history of lying or deceit will scare away others from dealing with him. This tells us that having a reputation of being just and truthful is a better recommendation than any sign or advertisement you might be able to create to promote your business.

There are excuses for lying that people sometimes give.

Some point their finger *at others*. They see people who lie everyday, even some who are known as good men. Therefore, they think it safe to do likewise. We have to admit, although it is a sad truth, that many, including professing Christians, are often guilty of lying. However, by using this line of reasoning as an excuse, that it is okay because others do it, we would find it acceptable to commit any number of crimes. When committed by professing Christians, this brings contempt upon God, and leads to general rebellion and disobedience to His will. Who is there that doesn't see the fallacy of such an excuse for lying?

Can you think that, because of their large number, those who are liars will somehow be protected from the wrath of God's infinite power and justice? Or that He will not honor His laws because of the large number of transgressors? Before you plead numbers as an excuse for iniquity and then find yourself trying to reconcile your anguish and seeking consolation amidst the flames of hell, remember that multitudes of "The wicked shall be turned into hell, and all the nations that forget God." (Psalms 9:17)

As we witness good men who fail in this way, let them be examples to us of caution, not imitation. They reveal to us the weakness of human nature and the necessity of constant watchfulness over ourselves. Let us remember the examples of falsehood given us in Scripture that were usually produced by fear rather than gain, as in the cases of Abraham, David, and Peter, among others. There is no doubt the souls of these men were deeply humbled by their recognition of this weakness in themselves. But these unusual cases give us no excuse to make a common practice of this vice. Do you think the omniscient God doesn't discern the occasional weaknesses of the upright heart from the perverse and willful disobedience of the rebellious heart? When you are seeking direction from examples in Scripture, don't omit the cases of Ananias and Sapphira, who both ended their lives with a lie (Acts 5).

Another excuse used is *the "smallness" of the sin*. Lying, they say, is not swearing, nor killing, nor stealing. This is to claim there can be no great harm in it because no great harm appears done by it. To this, we may reply that a sin is not little which produces men unlike the God of Truth, but more like the devil, the father of lies, which stands against the Authority of heaven, disturbs the peace of society, and which the good God sees fit to punish with bitter destruction.

If lying were so small a crime as some men want to believe it is, how many such small crimes can one bear? Is each small crime worthy of your attention, or only those you think concern the honor of God and the happiness of your own souls? The smallness of the sin that some use as an excuse is actually a collection of repeated crimes. If someone finds it too much to part with little sins, how can we expect them to part with those that are greater? Surely, he who will not deny a certain lust, so that his Lord and Savior may be pleased, will never lay down his life or part with his possessions when called to do so. Because they reveal less love towards God and concern to please Him, the habitual indulgence of little sins can be worse than committing a greater sin.

Others seek to excuse themselves of the sin by claiming it is just *a necessary part of doing business*. If true, that the lawful callings of life cannot be exercised with truth and a good conscience, this would indeed represent a significant problem! It would be to say that the righteous Governor of the universe has placed men in situations in life that conflict with His majesty and their own good consciences. We might then think it proper to write upon the door of every tradesman, as in times of trouble: "And I will strengthen the house of Judah, and I will save the house of Joseph, and I will bring them again to place them; for I have mercy upon them: and they shall be as though I had not cast them off: for I am the LORD their God, and will hear them" (Zechariah 10:6), while leaving such things as honor and integrity, religion and salvation, to those who are not employed in businesses.

Who can look at such things without seeing the fallacy in them, or without seeing how they misrepresent the will of the God of truth and goodness? How could they lift their face before heaven and say, "Lord God of heaven and earth, Thou knowest that from a sincere concern to please Thee and with a trust in Thy good providence, I have restricted myself to a high regard for truth in all my words and dealings. I appeal to Thee that I did not forsake the truth until I found poverty and ruin coming upon me, which I had no other way to prevent." Can you, in your conscience, plead for the necessity of lying, its practice and experience in your life? If not, then be ashamed to ever make such a plea. The claim that this sin is somehow necessary to doing business appears even more vain when one considers the truthfulness and veracity of many others in the same or similar business who are making a sufficient profit. I've spent a good deal of time focusing on this because it serves to address a number of other, similar excuses men make in an effort to silence the conviction of their own minds, encouraging themselves in vice and immorality.

On Honesty in Business

We'll now move on to considering how truth fits into our business activities. Being truthful does not require the tradesman to reveal every detail about his business, for example, the price that his goods cost him, where or how he obtains them, where his customers might find a lower price, or any of the lawful secrets that benefit his business. That is, although we may not lie for the purpose of deceiving or taking advantage of others, we may act in ways that protect our business from injury. We'll discuss these in more details now.

1. *Contracts and Promises*. This truth as it relates to the performance of all lawful contracts and promises. Prudence will help you to be cautious when making contracts and promises, so that they are equitable and suitable, as well as lawful and workable. Once you've made the commitment, although it may be difficult and costly, and although there may be no witnesses to them, God and conscience require you to make them good unless the other party or parties are willing to release you. Such agreements make up the bonds of human society that are necessary for men to confidently trust or trade with one another. The righteous man, though "He that sweareth to his own hurt, and changeth not." (Psalms 15:4). Who, then, can comfortably and safely operate a business that relies on faithless men, who have no regard for what they say or promise? We should also note that, if you enter into agreements on behalf of others, you are obligated to them as well.

This truth also requires workmen to accomplish their work in the time and manner they have promised, which is something that is often overlooked. The typical excuse is that something else interfered with the work, had a higher priority, or was more profitable. My response is that your promises should then include agreed-upon conditions. Otherwise, you may wrong one person in order to profit yourself or to please someone else. In situations that are truly unavoidable and to preserve a good conscience and character, you should do the best work you can in order to satisfy that customer. Just remember to be cautious of making hasty promises.

As mentioned before, there is no truth and justice when a man agrees on a trade but fails to follow through because of falling prices or some other contingency. Others, who promise to pay their bills or debts by such a date, neglect to do so or to even seek an extension for making payments. Such negligence, although seemingly minor to some, can lead to serious disruptions in society.

2. Product Representation. The matter of concealing material faults of a certain product is considered in the chapter on Justice. However, if you have any reason to believe that a customer will be disadvantaged by or have some other kind of problem with your products, the royal law of love and fairness requires that you warn them. In the same way, you should not be required to pay for that which is defective. If you're suspicious about the goodness or value of something, then you should plainly speak up. It is an unsound conclusion to claim that you have a right to take advantage of others because others have taken advantage of you.

3. Quality and Pricing. Truthfulness is demonstrated by not permitting your products to be over-rated, whether in quality or price. If you do this out of ignorance, you are still culpable, because you should not permit that of which you are not certain. However, if you know something you sell is being over-rated, particularly if you are the one doing it, then you are manifesting a breach of truth and justice.

One example of this occurs when someone pretends that his product is of a particular kind or from a particular country, when he knows it is not. Another is to claim that a product is faultless, when the faults are actually only covered up. Another is to say that a product was made by a certain highly-esteemed workmen and cost such a price, when it was neither one or the other. Yet another is to claim that you have already refused a certain price for it, when you know that the offer has never been made to you.

These and similar falsehoods, which some tradesmen often indulge themselves in, must certainly come from a hardened heart and a seared conscience. It is incredible that men who profess belief in an omniscient God and a future judgment of final retribution should dare to daily tell many lies for profit and thereby damn their souls, in order for them obtain that which, in the next moment, they wouldn't refuse to spend on their dogs.

Therefore, I encourage you not to pretend with respect to your religion and conscience. Don't dishonor the Christian name by falsely assuming it on yourself. Rather, admit what you truly are, either an atheist or an infidel. Change your practices and resolve, by the help of God, to be delivered from falsehoods, for "The getting of treasures by a lying tongue is a vanity tossed to and fro of them that seek death." (Proverbs 21:6).

4. *Your Opinions.* Being truthful is to also avoid making unjust criticism of people and things. When making a deal, buyers often say that something about the product is unimportant yet, when the purchase is over, they rejoice in getting something they said was unimportant. The guilt they feel over this is less than the gain they got by their deception and, by their words, they lie to their consciences. Although there are exceptional cases, we should generally be open about whether something is good or cheap. Otherwise, we wind up damaging our own sincerity and judgment.

It is right to complain of those things that are clearly either faulty or over-priced. However, when we only have doubts about a certain product, we should simply state those misgivings. Let the same attitude of carefulness and kindness be extended to all your fellow tradesmen. Be sure not to condemn his character or his goods without a just cause, or out of selfishness or malice. Remember that your words are not your own to simply enhance or criticize what you please. Rather, you are accountable to God for what you say, as you are for what you do.

5. *Your Communications.* Truthfulness in business excludes all attempts to cover up or to avoid responsibilities in our dealings with others. Our speech should be used to truthfully communicate with one another. When what we say is clouded with ambiguities or partial truths, especially with the intent to deceive, we defeat the purpose of communication and, in fact, manifest what is no better than a lie. What you say may be true in one sense but, in another, be false. This occurs when we say truthful things with wrong intentions, such as to coerce or deceive others, by knowing what they want to hear but not telling them everything they need to know. But this is as hateful and dangerous as a thief in disguise. Both are acting in ways contrary to truth and integrity, varying only in the nature of the falsehood. And both should be detested.

It is true that we are not always called to reveal everything we know about something, particularly when we are dealing with someone who is wrongly prying into our affairs or is actually conspiring against us. Just as the upright tradesman should be wise, he should also be truthful by saying what he thinks and doing what he says. It is too much like a scoundrel when our speech becomes like Apollo's oracles, where we may be understood in either a fair or a fatal sense. No one likes to be dealt with deceitfully, and no one should be deceitful towards others.

6. **Wordiness.** Our truthfulness helps to keep us from wordiness in our trading and conversations. Scripture censures wordiness as folly:

> "For a dream cometh through the multitude of business; and a fool's voice is known by multitude of words." (Ecclesiastes 5:3).
> "Seest thou a man wise in his own conceit? there is more hope of a fool than of him." (Proverbs 26:12).

Scripture also condemns wordiness as sin:

> "In the multitude of words there wanteth not sin: but he that refraineth his lips is wise." (Proverbs 10:19).

Yet, how often is a flood of words used to describe the most basic matters? Think of the common scenario where the seller asks for a price that is unreasonably high while the buyer offers a price that is unreasonably low. Ultimately, after much debate, they finally come to an agreeable price. But before that, one seeks to affirm that he will pay no more than a certain amount, while the other tries to settle for nothing less than some other amount, with both backing off from their words before they are done. Not every change of mind is a lie, and men may have a reason to change their minds when buying and selling. However, when they say one thing knowing they will shortly be contradicting what they just said, which I believe is usually the case, I cannot see how men can think they are not lying.

I am certain that, if men were not driven by greed on the one hand and injustice on the other, business deals might take place in two words rather than two hundred. Let the tradesman be content to make a reasonable profit, to be quick to set a price in the small things and, in the greater things (in order to conduct his business with ease and pleasure) to set a price or offer as close as possible to that which will establish a good reputation and secure a good conscience. A little determination and practice will make this easy. Many others have practiced this method with much success, and I'm satisfied that all who do so, from a principle of integrity and justice, will always be glad they did.

7. *Making Promises.* Truthfulness certainly helps us to exercise caution when making promises and to be careful to keep them. The breaking of promises, although common, is a significant crime. It represents a defiance of the God of heaven, it proclaims a person to be acting outside a rightful fear of God, and it is utterly destructive to human societies. When promises are broken, civil order and government is negatively impacted. It is not a breach of charity to think that a person who allows himself to become guilty of such things as perjury and faithlessness to also be capable of all imaginable evil. It is exceedingly evil in its nature and its consequences, bringing down the judgments of God on nations, families and persons. To those who commit it, it is the seed of self-tormenting desperation. Even heathens believe those guilty of it to be headed for destruction. Yet, how many nations today are groaning under the weight of this evil? What countless numbers of broken promises are continually committed to the horror and amazement of all caring people?

ON HONESTY TO CONSCIENCE

How foolish and absurd are they who expose themselves to the just resentment of heaven, who violate their own consciences and prostitute their reputations, by deceit and falsehood, in order to gain that which would be better secured by truth and integrity. This includes those things that offer no true satisfaction! The God of truth can never bestow His blessings on those who are in rebellion against Him, nor smile on what He abhors. In the end, what real comfort or good can men expect in their business dealings without the blessing of God? Does wealth enable men to be independent of God, and put them in a place above His just providence? Can He not bring sickness and losses, lay waste their plans, frustrate all their schemes for wealth and happiness, and cause them to "labour in the very fire, and the people shall weary themselves for very vanity?" (Habakkuk 2:13). After spending a lifetime of sorrow and disappointment here, can He not banish them to hell? Even if He permits their lying tongue, can the wealth gained by it be considered as anything but a dead weight that will sink them deeper into everlasting damnation? Where is reason and wisdom, even man's love of self, in pursuing a course with such dire consequences? If you value your own well-being, your internal comfort and your eternal happiness, be done with your lying.

Let truth and integrity rule in your places of business, and in your hearts. Let them be your constant companions in every business and activity. Recommend them to your children. Require them from your employees and helpers, for if you permit them to lie when it benefits you, they may not know how to avoid it when it does not. And, whenever you've not been truthful, express your concern by sincere repentance and change.

Here are some ways to help you deal honestly with your conscience as a tradesman:

1. *Restrain any covetousness you may have.* He that loves money more than God and conscience will displease both God and conscience. Covetousness is at the root of falsehood and many other vices.

2. Learn to trust God and His providence. This will set you apart from every wrong and unworthy plan, for he that believes in and depends upon God for all things will realize that a virtuous life is the means to God's blessings.

3. Never forget the exceeding wickedness and evil of lying. Men would not so readily commit sins of any kind if their consciences were not ignorant of the evil nature of sin.

4. Let the presence of God be a constraint to you whenever you're tempted to this sin. Surely, no one who considers himself in the continual presence of the God of truth can dare to deliberately lie. How can those who seek to deny His truth and omniscience during the day so easily then lift up their faces to Him in prayer at night?

5. Above all, be one who is always seeking to be renewed and sanctified by God's grace, laboring to attain a holy frame of mind. It is vain to attempt to purify the streams of vice while the fountain of iniquity (a corrupt nature) remains in all its vigor. But when cleansed by the precious blood of Jesus Christ and sanctified by the Spirit of God, only then will the result be pure and acceptable. A renewed conscience is the great preservative from all evil.

Conclusion

I have set before you the nature and necessity of truthfulness, and sought to inspire you to practice it. Only God knows what impression it has made upon your hearts, but this I must say: If you're not convinced by these arguments, God has one that will do so effectively, for He has said, "But the king shall rejoice in God; every one that sweareth by him shall glory: but the mouth of them that speak lies shall be stopped." (Psalm 63:11).

SCRIPTURE REFERENCES FOR CHAPTER 6

"Ye shall not steal, neither deal falsely, neither lie one to another." (Leviticus 19:11).

"Lord, who shall abide in thy tabernacle? who shall dwell in thy holy hill? In whose eyes a vile person is contemned; but he honoureth them that fear the LORD. He that sweareth to his own hurt, and changeth not." (Psalm 15:1,4).

"What man is he that desireth life, and loveth many days, that he may see good? Keep thy tongue from evil, and thy lips from speaking guile." (Psalm 34:12-13).

"Thou givest thy mouth to evil, and thy tongue frameth deceit. Thou sittest and speakest against thy brother; thou slanderest thine own mother's son. These things hast thou done, and I kept silence; thou thoughtest that I was altogether such an one as thyself: but I will reprove thee, and set them in order before thine eyes. Now consider this, ye that forget God, lest I tear you in pieces, and there be none to deliver." (Psalm 50:19-22).

"He that worketh deceit shall not dwell within my house: he that telleth lies shall not tarry in my sight." (Psalm 101:7).

"I hate and abhor lying: but thy law do I love." (Psalm 119:163).

"These six things doth the LORD hate: yea, seven are an abomination unto him: A proud look, a lying tongue, and hands that shed innocent blood," (Proverbs 6:16-17).

"The lip of truth shall be established for ever: but a lying tongue is but for a moment. Lying lips are abomination to the LORD: but they that deal truly are his delight." (Proverbs 12:19,22).

"A righteous man hateth lying: but a wicked man is loathsome, and cometh to shame." (Proverbs 13:5).

"A false witness shall not be unpunished, and he that speaketh lies shall not escape. A false witness shall not be unpunished, and he that speaketh lies shall perish." (Proverbs 19:5,9).

"Be not a witness against thy neighbour without cause; and deceive not with thy lips." (Proverbs 24:28).

"And they bend their tongues like their bow for lies: but they are not valiant for the truth upon the earth; for they proceed from evil to evil, and they know not me, saith the LORD. Shall I not visit them for these things? saith the LORD: shall not my soul be avenged on such a nation as this?" (Jeremiah 9:3,9).

"For the rich men thereof are full of violence, and the inhabitants thereof have spoken lies, and their tongue is deceitful in their mouth. Therefore also will I make thee sick in smiting thee, in making thee desolate because of thy sins." (Micah 6:12-13).

"These are the things that ye shall do; Speak ye every man the truth to his neighbour; execute the judgment of truth and peace in your gates:" (Zechariah 8:16).

"Ye are of your father the devil, and the lusts of your father ye will do. He was a murderer from the beginning, and abode not in the truth, because there is no truth in him. When he speaketh a lie, he speaketh of his own: for he is a liar, and the father of it." (John 8:44).

"And that ye put on the new man, which after God is created in righteousness and true holiness. Wherefore putting away lying, speak every man truth with his neighbour: for we are members one of another." (Ephesians 4:24-25).

"Lie not one to another, seeing that ye have put off the old man with his deeds;" (Colossians 3:9).

"For without are dogs, and sorcerers, and whoremongers, and murderers, and idolaters, and whosoever loveth and maketh a lie." (Revelation 22:15).

CHAPTER SEVEN

Of Contentment

> ... *the* LORD *gave, and the* LORD *hath taken away; blessed be the name of the* LORD.
> JOB 1:21

WITH REGARD TO THE TRADESMAN, CONTENTMENT represents a cheerful satisfaction with the place and calling God has given him. Some people, having a somewhat obstinate and self-sufficient temper, are more indifferent to the circumstances of life than others. But Christian contentment is a nobler thing. It arises from an appropriate sense of God's dominion over us, as our Lord and Owner who therefore may do with His own as He pleases. It expresses a humble trust in God as Father, whose wisdom and goodness directs by His grace everything He does towards us, in both the common things in life as well as the more pleasurable and profitable ones. This enables one to be content regardless of the situation they're in.

But, alas, where do we find this desirable virtue of contentment today? Men are usually not satisfied with their situation in life, and yearn for a change. Then, once they've made the change, they're as far from being happy as they were before.

Weary of being held back, children and employees often seek to be liberated from their parents or employers. Parents and employers, weary of the difficulties associated with their work, look forward to retirement. Those who are unmarried are frequently not content with their situation, while many of those who are married become even less content with theirs. The poor envy the wealth of the rich, while the rich admire the quiet and plain life of the poor.

Similarly, tradesmen are not free of restlessness. They often come to prefer other trades above their own. Indeed, ever since Adam became dissatisfied with the delights of paradise, all his posterity has been infected with this same unhappy disease. This continues until that time when God, by His grace, renews their nature, limits their desires, and shows them those things more lasting and substantial than the pleasures of the world, including the favor and enjoyment of His great and blessed Self.

EXAMPLES FOR THE TRADESMAN

Let's consider some examples where the tradesman is called to find contentment.

1. *In cheerfully handling the inconveniences and difficulties of his calling.* There are certain inconveniences common to most businesses. Indeed, none are truly free of them. For example, each tradesman is dependent upon many others. A mechanic will usually need to depend on many other experts. Those who are in commerce will often need to rely on many customers, including some who are indignant or arrogant, which try the patience of those in the trade.

Another inconvenience the tradesman often has to deal with are problem employees, such as those who tend to be lazy, careless, unfaithful, or even vicious. As soon as he turns his back, his business begins to fall apart: work is neglected, customers are slighted, and his goods embezzled. He finds himself losing more profit from within his place of business than he can bring in from the outside. Then there are all the different types of men he must meet and deal with. Some are liars and others deceitful.

In addition to the above inconveniences, there are those that relate to certain types of businesses. Some businesses require hard labor, and others continual attention. Other businesses are very active at certain times but then have little to do at other times. Such things can bring discontent to the tradesman. He may inwardly broil or outwardly flame to the point where he cries out, "Who would lead such a life as this?" or "Never was man so confused as this, or been such a slave!" Realizing that he is unable to reform others, he torments himself, is unable to find rest, and spends his time dwelling mostly on the miseries of his trade.

No one should think himself exempt from the common lot of mankind, or that the tempers and manners of men will change from what they've always been. Given our knowledge of our own shortcomings, we can't expect that those of others will suddenly disappear, or that we might somehow ride through the storms of life without being tossed about by its waves. It is best that we be patient with the matters of life and, realizing that we cannot make others better, we should be watchful that they not cause us to become anxious and impatient. Remembering that we have been placed in this world by divine providence, we should be certain to exercise our wisdom, patience and humility, in order to prepare us for a better place, and be contented with what we have.

2. *Focus on the good things.* Be content by being thankful for the good things about your callings, for God has given us what we need in the situations He has placed us. Therefore, we are not to be complainers. Those whose business is in the trading of various goods or products are usually involved in work that is less demanding physically than others. For example, the labor of a tradesman is less demanding than the work required of a husbandman, and less dangerous than that of a seaman. You're seldom kept from sleep by the aches and pains of daily labor. And, as a tradesman, you're usually not as exposed to variable weather conditions and other inconveniences as are others who support themselves and their families.

In some ways, the calling of the tradesman is often less stressful on the mind than others. It may provide you with more opportunity to study the Word of God, to learn from other books of instruction and through conversations with other men as well. You should take advantage of these opportunities. In addition, there are certain temporal advantages to being a tradesman. If God is pleased to add His blessing to your hard work, you may further enjoy additional provisions for both you and your family.

Lastly, the tradesman often has a better opportunity than others for doing good, which is among man's greatest honors and sources of happiness. You have the opportunity to educate and instruct those youth who work for you, to counsel them and to direct them regarding matters of religion and virtue. Through the grace of God, they may then learn those principles and habits that will benefit them and bless others around them in the future. In certain trades, many poor find employment, whose hard work may be a blessing to you and, if God prospers your business, you may then better serve their needs and those of others in the community as well. Indeed, many of the noblest charities today owe their foundations or continuation to the benevolence of mankind.

The tradesman should also be thankful for the many benefits of his particular calling, for every calling has its own special benefits as well as its own peculiar inconveniences. If the business requires a good amount of labor, it is often more free of certain types of concerns and less subject to financial loss. If it's a business that primarily deals in commerce, as in the buying and selling of goods, you will usually spend less time doing laborious work. If the business involves hazardous activity, the work is usually more profitable. If the tradesman takes note of such benefits in his business as these, he will conclude, "I am very happily situated, if I did but know it; and instead of envying the condition of others, or repining at my own, I only need a more thankful spirit for the blessings I enjoy."

3. *In business trials*. Through patience, the tradesman can find contentment during times of losses and disappointments in business. Sometimes the losses may be great because of the poor quality of the goods the tradesman deals in. At other times, it may be that his employees or partners are the source of problems. Storms and other adversities, as well as changes in the popularity of his goods, may be the source of financial losses.

In such situations, those with a discontented mind can become uneasy and confused. This can lead to severe business problems and a general contempt for all mankind because of the dishonesty of some. I fear that too often God's providence is blamed, if the tradesman doesn't already deny it because it does not favor his own plans. Thus, he neither enjoys nor gives God the praise for what he has, because he hasn't gotten everything he's wanted.

Christian contentment, although it isn't insensitive to financial losses, helps to absorb them. When situations are bad, they don't lead to depression or irresponsible behavior. The good man knows that constant happiness is found nowhere but in God and the testimony of a good conscience. The tradesman should realize that both difficult and prosperous times flow from the wisdom and goodness of his heavenly Father, and that the more humble and submissive he deals with the difficult times, the sooner he'll overcome them. During such times, he should give thanks to God for what he has and be compassionate toward others who might be similarly afflicted through no treachery of their own.

4. Beware of vice. Contentment can be maintained by monitoring those vices which conflict with it. We'll discuss what I mean by this with several examples.

Ambition

Ambition can cause the tradesman to aim at things beyond his abilities, making him restless and uneasy with his current situation. This can occur when his thoughts are too high for his calling or he hasn't achieved what he thinks is success. The shoe doesn't fit because the foot is swollen. Such dissatisfaction ruined our first parents, and it has led to fatal consequences for many of their children. Because of their foolish ambitions, many tradesmen have started businesses that then deprived them of the comfort they once enjoyed. It is reasonable that people should seek to improve their situation in life according to their abilities and the time available to them. However, it is not right for those desires and pursuits to lead them to become discontented and ungrateful for their present work, and interfere with their love and responsibilities to God and their neighbors. Instead of promoting the desires of benevolence and charity, ambition can encourage pride and a false sense of hope.

Envy

Here, we address the matter of men who become envious of the prosperity of others. One may think others less deserving of financial success than they, who are less diligent but somehow more successful. There are some who appear to live without much care or effort, yet all the riches they want just seem to easily flow towards them. The world is very unequally divided: some will work hard and be disappointed, while others will have a life of ease and wealth. Envy tells us to focus on that fine house, that expensive furniture, that growing business, and so forth, which someone else enjoys.

OF CONTENTMENT

A little modesty will remind you that the Governor of the universe knows best where to bestow His gifts, both for you and for your neighbor. If you truly seek the favor of the God of heaven, be content to be at His disposal. Be satisfied with what you have. You may not know the burdens of those you envy. You may see what seems to be their happiness but not see their miseries. You may not be aware of some of the cares, fears, or sorrows that can accompany financial wealth, along with the powerful temptations to pride, sensuality and forgetfulness of God that prosperity exposes one to. It might be that the people you envy need your compassion more than your emulation. "Be not thou afraid when one is made rich, when the glory of his house is increased." (Psalm 49:16). He that rejoices at the prosperity of others makes it his own. But he that envies it deprives himself of the comfort of what he possesses.

Covetousness

Covetousness is another vice that works against contentment. By covetousness, I mean an insatiable desire of wealth, when men think they cannot be happy unless they are rich. If the tradesman allows this desire into his heart he will become tormented by it. Because of his great desire to have more, he will not be able to find satisfaction with what he has. Because of this, he will worry over every little loss, and be filled with anguish over every disappointment. To gain wealth, he'll deny himself and his family of certain conveniences and necessities. His desire for wealth will be like the thirst from a fever: the more he drinks, the more he thirsts. How sad this is.

Riches don't make men more wise, happy or good. Neither do they help them develop good consciences or be employed to good purposes. Those who say they're seeking wealth is motivated by a desire towards kindness and charity should judge their sincerity by how they are using what they already have. We should not forget that those who are unfaithful with little will also be unfaithful with much. Similarly, a man who does not wisely employ a few talents will not be a good steward of many. If you neglect God's will for stewarding what He has given you, the pride and pleasures of life, as well as an increasing love of money, will interfere with your bearing the fruit of good works through increased wealth.

Man does not find true satisfaction through an increase of possessions but by managing his desires, for "He that loveth silver shall not be satisfied with silver; nor he that loveth abundance with increase: this is also vanity." (Ecclesiastes 5:10). Scripture, as well as experience, assures us that the happiness of man's life does not consist in the abundance which he possesses. Scripture tells us that, "...if riches increase, set not your heart upon them." (Psalm 62:10). Don't let your possessions possess you. Imitate the example of the good man, who said, "I take God to witness to my conscience. From Him, I desire no more in this world than that without which I cannot keep His laws."

Depression

Depression and a sense of hopelessness is another evil that interferes with contentment. This often happens to the tradesman when his business becomes monotonous or very slow. For example, he stocks his store with plenty of goods, but finds few customers for them. Or, he seeks or waits for business opportunities but finds only a few. Other tradesmen spend a lot of time and money on preparing or making the products they want to sell but don't know how to organize them for sale. They may even go into debt, or somehow seek to avoid the necessary expenses of their houses and families.

The tradesman should seek to develop an ability to look beyond the immediate horizon. His sense of hopelessness may have occurred because he lost sight of significant future opportunities after some current setbacks, not realizing that he can overcome these by applying some extra care and effort in his work for a while. Even amid his fears and gloomy expectations may the religious tradesman determine to persevere in diligence, frugality, and every necessary self-denial.

Let him, according to his conscience, use every prudent technique to strengthen his mind by trusting in God's promises and providence. May he believe that all things, even during times of gloom, are ordered by God in perfect wisdom and goodness, Who will never forsake those that fear and trust Him. Although God will sometimes bring men low, to humble and try them, and to teach them to be dependent upon Him, it is always for their good in the end. The Fountain of being and happiness can easily make up in spiritual blessings what may be lacking temporally. Therefore, when your spirits are down, continue to attend to the responsibilities of your work, and trust in God to ease your mind of any anxiety or worry you may have, dwelling on His Word: "And they that know thy name will put their trust in thee: for thou, LORD, hast not forsaken them that seek thee." (Psalm 9:10).

In the New Testament our Lord speaks similarly to the multitudes, "Therefore I say unto you, Take no thought for your life, what ye shall eat, or what ye shall drink; nor yet for your body, what ye shall put on. Is not the life more than meat, and the body than raiment? Behold the fowls of the air: for they sow not, neither do they reap, nor gather into barns; yet your heavenly Father feedeth them. Are ye not much better than they?" (Matthew 6:25-26).

A steadfastness in your calling, even under its inherent weaknesses, is another characteristic of the tradesman that brings contentment. There are many who, when they meet with some significant obstacle in their business, such as when business is very slow, are quick to seek after some other line of work. Others seem to never be able to find rest in any situation in life. Although we may form pleasing images of the benefits of other lines of work, we usually discover that, if we're not content with the calling we have prepared for, it will be unlikely we'll meet with better success doing something else. Therefore, people should be very cautious when they consider changes in the callings. They should make sure they have a good understanding of the nature of the new business, the skills or education needed, and a reasonable expectation of success in it. For this, they should seek the wisdom and experience of friends.

The problems that can arise from changing a trade often include the work environment, which may have earlier been one of the reasons for changing callings. Scripture addresses this when it says: "As a bird that wandereth from her nest, so is a man that wandereth from his place." (Proverbs 27:8).

God Desires Your Contentment

Let me emphasize the need and correctness of this amiable and happy disposition of contentment with the following observations.

1. *The Word of God commands us to be content.* "Let your conversation be without covetousness; and be content with such things as ye have: for he hath said, I will never leave thee, nor forsake thee." (Hebrews 13:5). No teaching could be more plain, nor any reason more powerful. Notice that in this verse we are told to, "be content with such things as ye have." What others have is not to be your standard. Their path may include more prosperity, and they may be better suited for it.

Your situation may be one where, in your earlier years, you lived better in some ways than you do today. And, because of this, you've become dissatisfied with your current situation. Perhaps, you've lost property to fire or had to provide for the many expenses of a large family. Be content with what you now have. Similarly one should not become discontented because they have not achieved or acquired what they desire. Don't say to yourself, "If I only had more business, less family expenses, fewer losses, or a better house, all would be well." For there is no virtue in being pleased when everything is only in our minds. Be cheerful and thankful in your present situation, realizing that you've been placed there by divine providence. God may have work for you to do and blessings for you to receive right where you are, which you are not aware of.

2. *It is not God's will for you to be discontent.* The blessed God is the Lord of the universe and the Absolute Disposer of all persons and things. Thus, because of His infinite wisdom and goodness, we can be assured that His will for us on this matter will not change, even though it may differ from our foolish desires and expectations. Is it reasonable to think that God should change His plan in order to satisfy the weak, shortsighted wishes of men?

That which appears to be harmful to me may be beneficial to many others. What cause have I to complain if the wind that dashes my ship against the rock at the same time may free two others from being stuck in the sand? Do we contradict our own prayers when we say, "Father, thy will be done" and then become satisfied when His will is done? If so, we would either be guilty of our hypocrisy in praying for something we do not truly desire or of our folly in contradicting our own wishes.

There are many other evils connected with a discontented mind that should deter us from it. It is evil in its causes, given that it comes from pride in the heart, envy, covetousness, distrust of God, and an ungrateful spirit for the many blessings we enjoy. It is also evil in its effects, in that it makes us unfit for the duties and pleasures of a spiritual life in Christ. People who are not satisfied with their lives are also not inclined to love and delight in God, or to praise and thank Him. Discontent tends to deform and disturb our own souls where, like oxen unaccustomed to the yoke, we become increasingly upset as we struggle against the burden, depriving ourselves of the true enjoyment of the blessings we have, yearning for that which we have not. In this way, we end up prolonging our troubles by interfering with the blessings that our heavenly Father is inclined to bestow on those who are humble and patient.

3. *If you are truly a Christian, you have the resources to be delivered from all discontent.* You have the perfections of God, the unsearchable riches of Christ, and the influence of the Holy Spirit of God. You have an interest in the promises of the Gospel, the divine image on your own souls, the infallible assurance of all that you need here on earth, and the hope and prospect of blessedness in the life to come. If these are not sufficient to satisfy you, I must say that you shamefully undervalue your many high privileges. "Bear your condition quietly, know that thou art a man," says the heathen philosopher. May I then say, "Be contented with your state, know that you are a Christian. You profess to live by faith, so do not behave otherwise."

4. *There is no condition of life, however low or difficult it may be, whereby God should not be honored in it and by it.* How you live your life, your patience, diligence and integrity, is a witness of your faith, not only to your peers, but to others as well. Those acts of charity and sacrifice that proceed from a heart of compassion and godliness, from a man willing to deny himself of many small pleasures in life, are more highly regarded by the Judge of all than the great monetary donations from the excess riches of the wealthy.

In consolation to the poor, let them consider that the lowest jobs are as necessary for the benefit and well-being of mankind as those that have a more impressive appearance. This is likened to a well-designed building, where not only are the beams and pillars necessary to its beauty and strength, but also the very nails. Common mechanic trades often contribute more to the well-being of a community than more refined employments, which often appear ornamental in many ways. May this be helpful to those whom providence has placed in the lowest situations in life, particular those who would compare their condition with others.

Paths to Contentment

Consider the following avenues to a happier disposition.

1. Keep an external perspective. Focus your mind on the reality and importance of a future condition. The man who thinks of himself as on earth only for a short time as part of an eternal existence, and finds himself battling for his soul with enemies within and without, will see the absurdity of being concerned about trivial matters in this life. I encourage you to evaluate the condition of your own soul. The mercy shown you and the righteousness you desire will serve to quench your thirst after other things. How deep is the passion of the sinful man, that he can be so continually and restlessly seeking after temporary and worthless things, while the image of God is lost in his soul and the anger of God ready to consume him!

2. Stay humble. If you wish to be content, seek to have a humble spirit. Pride causes men to be ungrateful for the mercy they receive and impatient under their crosses. But the one who is truly humble will easily bear afflictions and gratefully acknowledge blessings. The humble man recognizes that, although he may have a poor trade and a difficult condition, it could be worse. He might be begging or starving, or pining away in pain and misery. Yes, others may have more enjoyment of the temporal things of the world. But, the one who recognizes that he merits nothing of himself will be well contented with little.

3. *Seek moderation.* If you are to attain this happy state of contentment, learn to control and moderate your desires. "Nature and grace are contented with little, but pride and humor with nothing." The real needs of men are few and can quickly be supplied. But if all the things we merely desire or want somehow come to represent what we need, there will be no end to them. The only path to happiness is to find contentment with your situation in life, which is within the power of everyone by divine assistance. But few are they who achieve this. We find that when men have arrived at that place they thought would bring happiness, where their wealth is increasing, they are actually as discontented as ever. Therefore, if we have but a moderate lifestyle, we should be satisfied with it.

4. *Trust in God.* Lastly, you should seek to live a life that is dependent upon the blessings of God. When you place your happiness in His hands, you will easily be contented with whatever the world brings you. The soul that lives in fellowship with God and finds its happiness in Him will enjoy delights so noble and excellent that it will look with pity on the deluded world, which pursues the empty shadows of earthly happiness while neglecting the well-being of an immortal spirit. He who knows God, that all the perfection of God is engaged for his good, will be easily satisfied during every stage of life. Learn to be content with God's blessings and to accept His providence. Believe God to be both wise and good, to know what is best for you and willing to bestow it upon you, if you are careful to please Him. He who has

OF CONTENTMENT

promised glory and happiness in the end to those who love and fear Him will not deny them any necessary good on the way. Therefore, even in times of discouragement, seek to live according to His infallible word and promises, and you will certainly find that your hope was well placed.

SCRIPTURE REFERENCES FOR CHAPTER 7

"Then Job arose, and rent his mantle, and shaved his head, and fell down upon the ground, and worshipped, And said, Naked came I out of my mother's womb, and naked shall I return thither: the LORD gave, and the LORD hath taken away; blessed be the name of the LORD." (Job 1:20-21).

"But he said unto her, Thou speakest as one of the foolish women speaketh. What? shall we receive good at the hand of God, and shall we not receive evil? In all this did not Job sin with his lips." (Job 2:10).

"Rest in the LORD, and wait patiently for him: fret not thyself because of him who prospereth in his way, because of the man who bringeth wicked devices to pass. Cease from anger, and forsake wrath: fret not thyself in any wise to do evil. For evildoers shall be cut off: but those that wait upon the LORD, they shall inherit the earth. A little that a righteous man hath is better than the riches of many wicked." (Psalm 37:7-9,16).

"And they tempted God in their heart by asking meat for their lust. Yea, they spake against God; they said, Can God furnish a table in the wilderness? Behold, he smote the rock, that the waters gushed out, and the streams overflowed; can he give bread also? can he provide flesh for his people? Therefore the LORD heard this, and was wroth: so a fire was kindled against Jacob, and anger also came up against Israel; Because they believed not in God, and trusted not in his salvation" (Psalm 78:18-22).

"Better is little with the fear of the LORD than great treasure and trouble therewith." (Proverbs 15:16).

"Two things have I required of thee; deny me them not before I die: Remove far from me vanity and lies: give me neither poverty nor riches; feed me with food convenient for me: Lest I be full, and deny thee, and say, Who is the LORD? or lest I be poor, and steal, and take the name of my God in vain." (Proverbs 30:7-9).

"Better is the sight of the eyes than the wandering of the desire: this is also vanity and vexation of spirit. Seeing there be many things that increase vanity, what is man the better?" (Ecclesiastes 6:9,11).

"I form the light, and create darkness: I make peace, and create evil: I the LORD do all these things. Woe unto him that striveth with his Maker! Let the potsherd strive with the potsherds of the earth. Shall the clay say to him that fashioneth it, What makest thou? or thy work, He hath no hands?" (Isaiah 45:7,9).

"And he said unto them, Take heed, and beware of covetousness: for a man's life consisteth not in the abundance of the things which he possesseth. Consider the ravens: for they neither sow nor reap; which neither have storehouse nor barn; and God feedeth them: how much more are ye better than the fowls?" (Luke 12:15,24).

"Not that I speak in respect of want: for I have learned, in whatsoever state I am, therewith to be content." (Philippians 4:11).

"But godliness with contentment is great gain. For we brought nothing into this world, and it is certain we can carry nothing out. And having food and raiment let us be therewith content. But they that will be rich fall into temptation and a snare, and into many foolish and hurtful lusts, which drown men in destruction and perdition. For the love of money is the root of

OF CONTENTMENT

all evil: which while some coveted after, they have erred from the faith, and pierced themselves through with many sorrows. But thou, O man of God, flee these things; and follow after righteousness, godliness, faith, love, patience, meekness." (1 Timothy 6:6,11).

CHAPTER EIGHT
Of Religion

...Whosoever will come after me, let him deny himself, and take up his cross, and follow me.
MARK 8:34

IN THIS CHAPTER, I DON'T INTEND TO PROVIDE A FULL description of religion, since it includes topics already addressed elsewhere in this book, such as prudence, diligence, justice, integrity of speech, contentment, and so forth. Here, I primarily want to consider religion as it refers to our relationship with God. In this sense, it consists of having faith in and a correct understanding of God, as well as attitudes and practices that please Him. In Scripture this is often expressed by certain principles designed to influence our attitudes and lives, such as:

"...the fear of God." (Ephesians 5:21).
"...the love of God..." (2 Thessalonians 3:5).
"...the knowledge of God..." (2 Peter 1:2).
"...walk before God..." (Psalm 56:13).
"...with uprightness of heart..." (Psalm 119:7).
"...to be spiritually minded..." (Romans 8:6).

and the like.

However, such principles are not natural to man, whose mind is darkened by ignorance and whose affections are estranged from God and goodness. All man's powers and faculties are impaired and perverted by sin. The original righteousness of man is now contradicted by his sensual and evil appetites and affections. Such is the depravity of the human mind that, upon its conversion, men are said to:

> be "...born again..." (1 Peter 1:23).
> be made "...a new creature." (Galatians 6:15).
> be "...created in Christ Jesus unto good works..." (Ephesians 2:10).
> "...be renewed in the spirit of your mind." (Ephesians 4:23).

It is vain to attempt to heal the foolish things of the mind until the corrupt foundation of the cruel heart from which they come is purified. The tree must first be made good before the fruit from it can also be good. Our consciences must be purged from dead works and our souls united to Jesus Christ by a true and living faith before we can acceptably serve the living God.

How vain are all our confessions of sin, unless they flow from godly sorrow and a sincere faith in the great Redeemer's intercession and a true repentance before God? What are all our praises and thanksgivings to God, unless they proceed from a true love toward Him and gratitude for His mercies? What are our prayers and petitions but a mockery of His infinite majesty, unless they express the true and cheerful desire of our souls? And, how vain are all pretences of our love and reference of God, unless they are the product of a sincere and complete obedience to His will? In a word, in order for our work to be acceptable to God, it must be done according to His will. Such work cannot be done without a renewed soul, since "...the carnal mind is enmity against God: for it is not subject to the law of God, neither indeed can be." (Romans 8:7).

APPLYING OUR FAITH

Having laid the foundation for a religious life based upon faith in the Lord Jesus Christ and a right heart towards God, we can then move on to consider how to apply this faith.

1. Having a working knowledge of the attributes of God and our relationship with Him. God's glorious attributes will have a positive influence on us. Our response to His majesty and greatness is a humble reverence in all that we think or say about Him, and in the way we worship Him. Small or insignificant thoughts of God, the bold and irreverent use of His name, and careless expressions of worshipping Him are offenses to the infinite glory of His nature.

If we would serve God acceptably, it must be "...with reverence and godly fear: For our God is a consuming fire." (Hebrews 12:28-29). His unsearchable goodness and excellence claim our warmest affection and highest delight. To fix our greatest love on any lesser good is to slight and undervalue His glorious majesty, which could only come from an extraordinary perversion of judgment on our part.

God is not only the greatest good in Himself and the infinite fountain of all that is wise, amiable and good in the universe, but He is also the highest good for us and the only substantially satisfying delight of a reasonable immortal spirit. God therefore demands that "...thou shalt love the LORD thy God with all thine heart, and with all thy soul, and with all thy might." (Deuteronomy 6:5). We express our highest love for God in response to His nature, as we benefit and enjoy His blessings, and as we continually partake of His goodness and depend upon His favor.

The purity and holiness of God, as the foundation of our reverence and esteem, give us a humbling sense of our own guilt and depravity. This causes us to fly to the grace and Spirit of our adorable Redeemer for the pardon of our guilt and the healing of our natures, never resting until we become holy as He is holy. The omniscience of God should encourage us to watch over the conditions of our hearts, and discourage us from all pretense and hypocrisy in both spiritual matters and our dealings with men. Indeed, we should act as being continually in the presence and under the watchful eye of that God, believing His word that "Neither is there any creature that is not manifest in his sight: but all things are naked and opened unto the eyes of him with whom we have to do." (Hebrews 4:13). Lastly, we should always be ready and willing to abide by the promises and curses revealed to us by God through His word.

Likewise, our relationship with God requires that we maintain a proper attitude and behavior toward Him. As creatures, we should never forget that He is our absolute Lord. We are His much more that anything we possess is ours, since we've only derived a right from Him to all that we enjoy. Therefore, it is essential that we yield ourselves to Him so that we may be used for His purposes. As we commit ourselves to a complete obedience to His will, we are assured that He will preserve and bless us, and employ us in ways that will return us to a condition infinitely better than the one He found us in. We should remember that "...ye are not your own" (1 Corinthians 6:19).

We are also called to "...glorify God in your body, and in your spirit, which are God's." (1 Corinthians 6:20). As our Preserver and Benefactor, we should trust in His goodness and resign ourselves to His care. Be one who seeks God continually for all the blessings you need. Maintain a sense of gratitude, always acknowledging thankfulness to Him, for all benefits we receive are from Him. Be one that expresses this from your heart and in your life. These are our obligations, confirmed by the light of nature, towards God, our sovereign Lord and Creator.

However, we're creatures who have in numerous instances violated God's holy law, presenting ourselves repulsive before His pure and unspotted nature. Thus, all hope of His favor and acceptance would have ended if, in His infinite goodness and mercy, He had not offered Himself to us a Redeemer and Sanctifier. This is the great design of the gospel of Christ that proposes to all who, realizing their guilt and just punishment, sincerely embrace Him as their Savior.

For our own safety and happiness, these things should cause us to reflect with shame and sorrow upon our disobedience and rebellion against God, to fly for refuge from His just vengeance to Jesus Christ as the only Redeemer for sinners. We must put our trust in His sacrifice and mediation to obtain our acceptance with God. We seek to live as His disciples by imitating His holy life, attending to His doctrines (as the great Teacher and Restorer of mankind) and obeying His heavenly precepts (as the universal Lord and Head of His Church). In order to do this, we need the help of the Holy Spirit to sanctify and renew our natures, to restore the image of God lost in our souls, and to give us the attitude of His adopted children. This working knowledge of God will impact the whole frame of our hearts and lives.

2. Religion includes our obedience to the Word of God as the guiding principle of our faith and practice. Our reverent regard of the Holy Scriptures and our humble submission to them is an inseparable result of true religion. The one who is truly of God will be both a hearer and doer of God's word, and be directed by it in every situation and circumstance of life. The more we study the Word and the closer we adhere to it, the wiser and happier we'll be.

Whenever there is a departure from the guiding principles of

THE RELIGIOUS TRADESMAN

God's Word, we find ignorance, folly and unhappiness. Without exception, an unchanging rule is that the more we have been influenced by the Spirit and virtuous living, the more we'll esteem and love the blessed records of the Holy Scriptures. We might venture to declare that the neglect of the Bible is the principle cause for all the profanity and immorality of the present age. This is one more reason why the religious tradesman should not allow himself to become governed by the examples of the humor, desires, and selfish views of others but, rather, by the Bible.

I tend to believe that many of the problems associated with poor decisions by tradesmen would have been prevented if they had walked more in line with God's Word. "Bind them continually upon thine heart, and tie them about thy neck. When thou goest, it shall lead thee; when thou sleepest, it shall keep thee; and when thou awakest, it shall talk with thee. For the commandment is a lamp; and the law is light; and reproofs of instruction are the way of life." (Proverbs 6:21-23).

3. *The tradesman's religion exists in living by faith in God through all the many changing conditions of an unpredictable world.* Like an anchor, his faith will keep his soul quiet and peaceful during all the storms of life. It will also serve to enliven his hope, energize his work, and help him in every situation. "Thou wilt keep him in perfect peace, whose mind is stayed on thee: because he trusteth in thee." (Isaiah 26:3). How contrary to this is the state of every ungodly, worldly mind! If the world smiles upon him, he'll tend to idolize it, but if the world frowns upon him, he'll become depressed. Since all his hopes and treasures are of this world, his sense of well being will fluctuate as the world fluctuates, that is, his focus will be on temporal prosperity.

On the other hand, a good man, although not indifferent to prosperity or adversity in the world, won't be anxious for anything. "He shall not be afraid of evil tidings: his heart is fixed, trusting in the LORD." (Psalm 112:7). After all, what are all of the important matters of Christianity without faith, which is "...the substance of things hoped for, the evidence of things not seen." (Hebrews 11:1). Without faith, what influence will the Word or worship of God have on us? In short, we must be people who live by faith and breathe by prayer.

4. Another important part of the Christian's life is serious and constant worship of God. The same light that reveals the Being of God to us also tells us that it's our essential duty to worship Him. This truth is so deeply impressed upon the mind of man that no one except the degenerate who falsely professes faith in Christ neglects in some way or another to pay adoration to God by their worship. This is the tradesman's duty, as well as others, for how can those who never come near to God be said to be where he should be. "Brethren, let every man, wherein he is called, therein abide with God." (1 Corinthians 7:24). We draw near to God by meditation and prayer, and by His Living Word. Surely, creatures whose happiness depends on God shouldn't need further argument to persuade them to be continuously seeking Him. "And when they shall say unto you, Seek unto them that have familiar spirits, and unto wizards that peep, and that mutter: should not a people seek unto their God? for the living to the dead?" (Isaiah 8:19).

However, the tradesman's religious worship shouldn't be restricted to the church meeting or the closet. For instance, there are family needs to be fulfilled, family sins to be forgiven, and family blessings to be thankful for. Family worship is then a necessary duty for him. On the other hand, we find the families who are the subjects of Divine vengeance to be those "...who eat up my people as they eat bread, and call not upon the LORD." (Psalm 14:4). Therefore, find time in the morning and evening to bring your thoughts and concerns before God. Don't let company or business keep you from both regular and special prayer time with God. Remember that God calls you to pay Him your first and highest attention. Let nothing interfere with your worship and devotion time except that which is a higher and necessary calling. Don't use the excuse that you've no time for it, for men always make time to eat and sleep regardless of what business is left undone because of it. Nothing is more necessary, and has fewer excuses for avoiding, than worship.

It may be that you only need an hour a day for devotions and worship because it's not the length but the sincerity of the worship that makes them acceptable to God. Certainly, He expects you to find time for such an important matter. Don't plead that your work leaves you in the evenings without the strength or spirit for it, for devoting too much time and energy to your work may be as wrong as eating too much. God won't bless such eagerness in business when it interferes with His other callings to you. And, of course, you can't use such an excuse in the mornings, given that your spirits are then fresh and vigorous.

The greater problem in such situations isn't whether one is able to find the time and energy to worship God but, rather, whether one wants to worship Him. It's more reasonable for us to simply say that, since we have labored all day long for food and shelter and clothing, shouldn't we now exert ourselves in the evenings for the blessing of God's forgiveness and grace? Shouldn't we now stretch forth our souls for the eternal crown? O, don't let your hard work and eagerness for the treasures of this world cause you to become lax in seeking heavenly riches. Give each their due attention and place in your heart and your work.

5. *Another part of the Christian faith is the religious observance of the Lord's Day,* being one of the first things changed by the grace of God in the sincere Christian. As the tradesman begins to look earnestly towards God and heaven, he comes to value and occupy this day in a different manner than he did before. To the extent that faith flourishes in the soul, so does his esteem of this sacred time. Be one who remembers the Sabbath day before it comes, endeavoring to clear your mind of worldly cares and obstacles, so that you're prepared to make best use of that day. Prepare yourself to be ready to adore and praise the majesty and qualities of God, to celebrate and seek the blessings of redeeming love and grace through Jesus Christ our Lord, to hear His most holy Word and receive instructions from it, and to acknowledge His mercies toward you with gratitude and joy. Be ready to lament and confess the sins and foolishness of your heart and life with sincere sorrow and contrition.

In short, as the Lord's Day approaches, ready yourself to receive and strengthen those characteristics of holiness that will prepare you for a wise, satisfying and religious life on earth, and the glories of an everlasting state in the world to come. Don't let the love or guilt of any sin be a part of this day. Pray: "I will wash mine hands in innocency: so will I compass thine altar, O LORD" (Psalm 26:6). Although it's good and right to be cheerful with holy joy on the Lord's Day, be careful to avoid the sensual pleasures, as well as vain and fruitless thoughts and conversations. Avoid worldly business activities or discussions, which could have taken place earlier on or may be done at some future time. "If thou turn away thy foot from the sabbath, from doing thy pleasure on my holy day; and call the sabbath a delight, the holy of the LORD, honourable; and shalt honour him, not doing thine own ways, nor finding thine own pleasure, nor speaking thine own words:" (Isaiah 58:13). Think of how great a blessing it is that you're given the opportunity to approach God, and time to prepare your soul for eternity, and improve it as needed.

Don't exclude your families from these benefits. In fact, this is one of the reasons why we should avoid the common business activities on the Lord's Day. Be sure to give your employees sufficient time for the worship of Almighty God. Don't allow their souls to go unnourished for the sake of helping you feed you and your family. You should not only allow your children and employees time for religious activities but you should seek to instruct them in matters of religion and virtues, encourage them in what's good, and seriously correct that which is not proper in them. You treat them worse than your own cattle if you allow them to travel upon paths that typically lead to misery and destruction without doing anything about it. Don't let up on them until they're either delivered from their ignorance, by God's grace, or they're found to be incurable.

Also, remember that it's "...the sabbath of the LORD in all your dwellings." (Leviticus 23:3). So, the Lord should be honored and served, not only in places of public worship, but everywhere. Read His Word with reverence and attention, sing His praises with understanding and delight, and seek His favor with humility, faith and sincerity. Do this to help prepare yourself for the heavenly kingdom and for carrying the blessings of God into the work of the new week. A good and great man once observed that, in his experience over many years, he had found that giving proper attention to activities on the Lord's Day had always brought blessings upon the remainder of the week. But, when he neglected such duties, he always had problems at his own secular work during the week. By the way, this wasn't the conclusion from a single observation.

6. *Another important component in Christian life is the habit and practice of religious conversation.* That is, to apply the noble faculty of speech in a way that reflects your faith and serves as a good witness to others. "The mouth of the righteous speaketh wisdom, and his tongue talketh of judgment. The law of his God is in his heart; none of his steps shall slide." (Psalm 37:30-31). We should especially be careful to avoid hurtful talk, which poorly reflects upon the honor of the blessed God and tends to lessen men's regard for Him. Such talk includes that which defiles and corrupts the mind, harms the reputation of others not present, and provokes or insults those who are. Such is the result of idle, empty, or vain conversation. We should banish from our lives whatever speech is contrary to our faith, to charity, or to chastity. In addition to abstaining from hurtful discussions, we should strive to have useful, meaningful ones.

As in other parts of the Christian character, the tongue of man was given to him to be used in ways that praise his Maker, and that are useful and instructive to those around him. The angels themselves have no nobler or more delightful opportunities for such praise than do we. Such praise could well include: the glorious perfection of God; the amiable Jesus; the holy Word of God; His wondrous works of nature, providence, and grace; the happiness of the eternal world before us; the means and help to our safe arrival there, and fitness for it; and the dangers, follies, and snares that lie in our way. Now, there are topics most worthy of discussion! It would be foolish to sneer at their being spoken of at any appropriate situation, or to think that the weather, the neighbor's behavior or a thousand other similar subjects, would be more beneficial to man's rational soul or immortal nature.

I realize that we have certain lesser, more mundane, subjects that need to be considered while we are still in this world, and that we need to devote some of our thoughts and words to talking about them. It is also not best for us to spend all our time analyzing every profane thing according to Scripture. However, to suggest that Christians should avoid religious conversation because someone finds it melancholy or mean is as absurd as suggesting that the world is more important than God, or money than heaven, and basic worldly pleasures more worthy than grace and glory. Are the sneers of one who would say such things worse than hell or sin?

7. *Another important part of Christian practice is pious meditation, where we discern our spiritual state by reflecting on our current thoughts.* People filled with greed for example, will constantly be thinking about getting riches. Others, filled with certain lusts of the flesh or eyes, will be thinking about how to gratify their senses. Those who are very ambitious will be thinking of how to gain the approval of men. However, since the hopes and happiness of the sincere Christian center on God and His favor, he'll be frequently and seriously thinking about that which helps him focus on and enjoy God. One of the infallible principles of the One who formed the spirit of man and knows how it operates is "where your treasure is, there will your heart be also." (Matthew 6:21). While the hands of the pious tradesman are employed in the common business of life, his heart will be aspiring to God, delighting itself in His attributes, His Word, and His works. As no ship is so full that it cannot contain many more jewels, no business can so occupy our minds as to not allow for serious thought of God. It isn't necessary for us to go off to a retreat to exercise a religious attitude of mind or lead a virtuous life.

Our meditations should be thought of as the means to positively influence and affect our souls. We're to be thinking about those subjects that should be important to us, until we receive direction. We should meditate on the great and important truths, as they're usually the surest and least prone to confuse us. These include the attributes of God, His wonderful love and goodness as revealed in Jesus Christ, the great seriousness of a future judgment, the importance and certainty of an eternal state of existence, and the shortness and uncertainty of time. Meditation on these truths will, by the grace of God, produce a holy life.

OF RELIGION

Sometimes, our meditations may include spontaneous prayers and addresses to heaven, such as that by Nehemiah, who said, "...Remember me, O my God, for good." (Nehemiah 13:31). Or of the royal Psalmist who wrote, "I am thine, save me: for I have sought thy precepts." (Psalm 119:94). When you feel the guilt of sin pressing on you, or the sense of mercy affecting you, or any difficulty or danger scaring you, such verses as these will provide comfort to your spirit until more devotional time arrives. It can sometimes help to consider our thoughts as part of a conservation we have with ourselves, either stirring us up out of our laziness or comforting our depressed souls, or perhaps by pleading with our own hearts for conviction. The Psalmist says, "Why art thou cast down, O my soul? and why art thou disquieted within me? hope thou in God: for I shall yet praise him, who is the health of my countenance, and my God." (Psalm 42:11). Having rebuked his fears as unreasonable, his faith revives, and he places his hope in God, while seeking to praise Him.

Lastly, it's important to learn from the great variety of useful reflections drawn from everyday events and activities in life. For example, the sudden death of someone may quicken us in preparing for our own death, and reveal to us the vanity of earthly pursuits. The sight of those who are deformed or miserable may help to teach us gratitude to God for His goodness to us. When we see the many dangers and extreme effort that others undergo for some small financial benefit, this may help deliver us from our negligence in our pursuit of heaven and eternal happiness. Indeed, there are very few observations we make that we can't also learn or benefit from in some way. This, no doubt, is behind the design for the many similes and parables in the Word of God, that we might be instructed by familiar objects or situations. We're sent to the ant to learn about wisdom and hard work, to the potter to be taught about submission, to the will of God, and to the refiner to receive comfort and instruction under affliction.

For the same purposes, the Gospel is filled with many symbols, among which are: the vine, the fig tree, the costly pearl, the persistent widow, and the prodigal son. How beneficial to the religious tradesman if he would, like the industrious bee, be gathering nectar from every flower. How sad it is when Christians, who should know how to converse with men and sometimes even with God Himself, are at a loss in how to properly commune with their own hearts.

8. The practice of our faith requires that we always remain watchful. Whenever there is sincere love and fear of God, there will be a constant desire to please Him. This can never be achieved by imperfect beings with strong appetites and passions amid the many temptations to evil from an ensnaring world and vigilant spiritual adversaries, unless we're watchful and in prayer regarding every temptation. The Christian should be particularly watchful regarding those sins to which his calling exposes him. The sure sign of an upright heart is that we're keeping ourselves from our own iniquity. This refers to that which we're inclined to, which we find most difficult to resist and hardest to overcome, for which our conscience most frequently rebukes us and we condemn ourselves when afflicted.

The vices we're all most prone to include pride, greed and the lust of the flesh and eyes. Therefore, the tradesman should be especially watchful for signs of them. They're at the root of all kinds of evil. They deaden the affections toward God and goodness. They sensualize the very souls of men, and give such a lawless bias to their appetites, that they produce forgetfulness and contempt of God. They lessen the desire for purity and spirituality of God's laws and worship, and cause people to neglect their immortal souls and concerns of another world. They cloud our understanding, pervert our judgment, and extinguish the principles of religion, justice, truth and benevolence in the hearts of men.

Such things are frequently mentioned throughout Scripture as to be absolutely inconsistent with Christian life and destructive of our heavenly hopes. "For this ye know, that no whoremonger, nor unclean person, nor covetous man, who is an idolater, hath any inheritance in the kingdom of Christ and of God." (Ephesians 5:5). We also read, "For they that are after the flesh do mind the things of the flesh; but they that are after the Spirit the things of the Spirit. For to be carnally minded is death; but to be spiritually minded is life and peace. Because the carnal mind is enmity against God: for it is not subject to the law of God, neither indeed can be. So then they that are in the flesh cannot please God. For if ye live after the flesh, ye shall die: but if ye through the Spirit do mortify the deeds of the body, ye shall live." (Romans 8:5-8,13).

A Personal Check-up

Now that we've considered various examples of the practice of a Christian attitude and life, let's search ourselves and consider what our own attitudes and practices have been. Have we truly experienced a renewing of the mind that has inclined our soul towards God and Christ, heaven and holiness? Or, are we the same self-righteous, sensual, dead, and rebellious beings towards God and goodness that we always were? Have the glorious attributes of the adorable God and our relationship before Him had a real and habitual impact on our lives? Or have we ignored the God who made us, neglected to glorify that Transcendent and Supreme Being in whose hand our breath is, and lightly esteemed the Lord Jesus Christ, the Rock of our salvation? Have we studied and reverenced the holy Word of God and made it the rule and guide of our lives? Or, have we made the customs and examples of an evil world or our own selfish interests and desires the rule for our behavior? Have we lived by faith in God for all we need in life? Or, have we put our faith in the treasures of this world? Has our worship of the Almighty been performed with seriousness, faith and consistency in our families and devotions? Or have we lived as without God in the world and cast off fear by restraining our prayers before Him? Have we honored, reverenced, and delighted in the Lord's Day? Or have we viewed it as a distraction from the common business and pleasures of the world? Have we been watching over what we've said? Has our conversation been sober, rational, useful, and religious? Have our hearts been frequently seeking God, by serious reflection and meditation, so that our souls might be energized and strengthened by God? Or has vanity and foolish thoughts and words been so dear to indicate absence of a wise and religious inclination of heart and temper of mind in us?

In conclusion, have we been watchful and careful in our Christian life, especially in regard to the predominant sins of covetousness and sensuality? Or have our souls been buried in the earth, or drowned in carnality, as we've ignored God, Christ and the eternal world? These are serious questions we need to put before our consciences, while there is time to repent, before we are called into the presence of God, from Whose judgment there is no appeal. His examination of our hearts and lives will be more particular and exact than any we could perform.

THOSE WHO OBJECT TO A RELIGIOUS LIFE

Let me address some of those matters that arise in the minds of men against a religious life. One is the claim that it's too difficult, that the rules are too self-denying, and that the path to heaven is so narrow that one can't also be comfortable and happy. To this it might be said that there's nothing that God requires or forbids that does not also contribute to the true happiness of His creatures. Instead, it's the excessive indulgence of animal appetites that destroys true peace and the purity of the human mind, rather than the restrictions placed on them by God. If our corrupted natures find rules that cause them to be restrained, can we think our appetites and affections so wise as to know when they need to be restrained? Or, if we arrive at a place with a certain kind of happiness, thinking that the work was too hard or our self-denial too great, shall we repent then? Surely not! There is nothing so hard in the Christian life that, by the grace of God and virtuous habits, won't be made easier for us. Some of the greatest struggles in the Christian walk are at first, before the mind has been healed of its dominant illnesses. However, the longer we travel the path, the more sweet and delightful is the journey. Many things in life appear difficult when we first encounter them. So, why should we be alarmed when confronted with the difficulties of following Christ?

There are some who claim that the rules and self-discipline are more than what should be required. In reply, we simply need to consult the holy Scriptures by which we're to be judged. Let's see whether "...denying ungodliness and worldly lusts..." (Titus 2:12) is not everywhere made the qualification for enjoying the next world. Then, we should consider what we should believe: the words from the dark and depraved mind of man, or the declarations of infinite wisdom, goodness, and truth.

There are some perhaps who aren't willing to follow Christ because they think it may expose them to contempt by others. To them, I ask, What is there that merits contempt regarding the belief, reverence and love of the God of heaven and earth, in acknowledging your dependence on Him, and expressing your gratitude to Him by humble prayer and praise? Or in regard to goodness, truth and justice toward man, and in the moderating of your appetites and passions? Yet, these are the substance of the practice of Christianity. It's by these, the noblest and most blessed of things, that you're afraid of being embarrassed. One of the wisest heathens said, "That virtue was so beautiful that if it could be rendered visible to the eyes of man, everyone would be in love with it." Where Christianity isn't maimed or deformed by those who profess it, it commands respect and reverence from those who witness it. I have no doubt that the most ruinous and extravagant man now on earth would readily give ten thousand worlds if he had them to give, if only his life had been lived strictly conformed to the wise and holy will of God. Which then deserves our greatest attention: the approval of God, of angels and of all good men, or the criticisms of those who'll soon condemn themselves for neglecting what they now despise? "And when he had called the people unto him with his disciples also, he said unto them, Whosoever will come after me, let him deny himself, and take up his cross, and follow me. Whosoever therefore shall be ashamed of me and of my words in this adulterous and sinful generation; of him also shall the Son of man be ashamed, when he cometh in the glory of his Father with the holy angels." (Mark 8:34,38).

A Religious Life Recommended

We should note that a life of serious, practical religion is recommend to us by those matters which are most important. Let's look at some of them.

1. *It represents true wisdom.* Some may claim that the wisest man is the one who, after serious attention and much foresight, secures the most good for himself while he escapes the greatest evil. Since heaven is a better place than is this fallen world, and eternity longer than time, how much wiser is he who, by faith in Christ Jesus, and conformity to the prescribed rules of the Gospel, obtains its invaluable blessings, than he that gains the greatest worldly good. If God, the Fountain of Wisdom, is the proper Judge, we already have His decision in His Word, "And unto man he said, Behold, the fear of the LORD, that is wisdom; and to depart from evil is understanding." (Job 28:28). How vain is the man who pretends to be wise, regardless of all his wealth, wit, or learning, whose mind is alienated from God, whose eternal well-being is neglected, in return for the dreams and shadows of worldly pursuits and pleasures.

2. *A life of religion provides the truest happiness.* There's nothing that so greatly contributes to the well-being of the soul, and crowns it with peace and tranquility, as the faith in and the fear of God, a supreme affection to Him, and a relationship with Jesus as Lord and Savior. The delights of a sincere Christian faith so greatly surpass the pleasures of the covetous, the sensual and lustful, as the pleasures of man do those of the beasts. If the blessed God represents the happiest Being, then those that bear closest resemblance to Him must necessarily be the happiest creatures. Not only do they benefit from and enjoy the divine pleasures of a religious life but are most truly satisfied with the blessings they have in common with other men. Our Christian faith doesn't constrain us from those pleasures that are consistent with reason and our well-being. Nothing else can provide the same comfort under the unavoidable afflictions in this life. I may venture to claim that even the remorseful sorrow of a good man may have more true satisfaction in them than the greatest delights that the wicked and profane ever enjoyed.

3. *True Christianity is the greatest necessity.* Compared with this, every other concern is as the toys of children to the labors of life. This is the one thing needful, without which the end of created man is lost, the glory of God in His works is frustrated, and the whole existence of mankind is in vain. It would have been better to have never been created than to leave this world with the guilt of sin unpardoned, and its power unconquered. It's also necessary to obtaining a blessing upon all our temporal needs as well. Godliness comes with it the promise of life, in this world and in the one to come. God will bless all who truly serve Him. Men may increase their riches by other methods, but the prosperity of such fools only tends to destroy them. If we neglect our love and responsibilities towards God, He can easily thwart our most vigorous effort for the things of this life. The tradesman would do well to consider whether many of his losses or failures might not be a chastisement for his neglect of these important concerns.

SCRIPTURE REFERENCES FOR CHAPTER 8

"For this commandment which I command thee this day, it is not hidden from thee, neither is it far off. That thou mayest love the LORD thy God, and that thou mayest obey his voice, and that thou mayest cleave unto him: for he is thy life, and the length of thy days: that thou mayest dwell in the land which the LORD sware unto thy fathers, to Abraham, to Isaac, and to Jacob, to give them." (Deuteronomy 30:11,20).

"Wherefore the LORD God of Israel saith, I said indeed that thy house, and the house of thy father, should walk before me for ever: but now the LORD saith, Be it far from me; for them that honour me I will honour, and they that despise me shall be lightly esteemed." (1 Samuel 2:30).

"Only fear the LORD, and serve him in truth with all your heart: for consider how great things he hath done for you. But if ye shall still do wickedly, ye shall be consumed, both ye and your king." (1 Samuel 12:24-25).

"And Solomon said, Thou hast shewed unto thy servant David my father great mercy, according as he walked before thee

OF RELIGION

in truth, and in righteousness, and in uprightness of heart with thee; and thou hast kept for him this great kindness, that thou hast given him a son to sit on his throne, as it is this day." (1 Kings 3:6).

"Blessed are they that keep his testimonies, and that seek him with the whole heart. Thou hast commanded us to keep thy precepts diligently. I have rejoiced in the way of thy testimonies, as much as in all riches. Depart from me, ye evildoers: for I will keep the commandments of my God. Salvation is far from the wicked: for they seek not thy statutes. LORD, I have hoped for thy salvation, and done thy commandments." (Psalm 119:2,4,14,115,155,166).

"In the way of righteousness is life: and in the pathway thereof there is no death." (Proverbs 12:28).

"Whoso despiseth the word shall be destroyed: but he that feareth the commandment shall be rewarded." (Proverbs 13:13).

"And now also the axe is laid unto the root of the trees: therefore every tree which bringeth not forth good fruit is hewn down, and cast into the fire. Whose fan is in his hand, and he will throughly purge his floor, and gather his wheat into the garner; but he will burn up the chaff with unquenchable fire." (Matthew 3:10,12).

"Not every one that saith unto me, Lord, Lord, shall enter into the kingdom of heaven; but he that doeth the will of my Father which is in heaven." (Matthew 7:21).

"Then said they unto him, What shall we do, that we might work the works of God? Jesus answered and said unto them, This is the work of God, that ye believe on him whom he hath sent." (John 6:28-29).

"And herein do I exercise myself, to have always a conscience void of offence toward God, and toward men." (Acts 24:16).

"What fruit had ye then in those things whereof ye are now

ashamed? for the end of those things is death. But now being made free from sin, and become servants to God, ye have your fruit unto holiness, and the end everlasting life. For the wages of sin is death; but the gift of God is eternal life through Jesus Christ our Lord." (Romans 6:21-23).

"For this is the will of God, even your sanctification, that ye should abstain from fornication: For God hath not called us unto uncleanness, but unto holiness." (1 Thessalonians 4:3,7).

"Looking for that blessed hope, and the glorious appearing of the great God and our Saviour Jesus Christ; Who gave himself for us, that he might redeem us from all iniquity, and purify unto himself a peculiar people, zealous of good works." (Titus 2:13-14).

"Though he were a Son, yet learned he obedience by the things which he suffered; And being made perfect, he became the author of eternal salvation unto all them that obey him;" (Hebrews 5:8-9).

"Follow peace with all men, and holiness, without which no man shall see the Lord: Looking diligently lest any man fail of the grace of God; lest any root of bitterness springing up trouble you, and thereby many be defiled;" (Hebrews 12:14-15).

"But the day of the Lord will come as a thief in the night; in the which the heavens shall pass away with a great noise, and the elements shall melt with fervent heat, the earth also and the works that are therein shall be burned up. Seeing then that all these things shall be dissolved, what manner of persons ought ye to be in all holy conversation and godliness," (2 Peter 3:10-11).

CHAPTER NINE

Of Leaving *our* Callings

If a man die, shall he live again? all the days of my appointed time will I wait, till my change come.
JOB 14:14

HERE, IN THIS FINAL CHAPTER, I'M GOING TO DISCUSS those situations where it may be appropriate for someone to leave their calling. There are, of course, those important situations where it may be necessary for a tradesman to be detained or diverted from his business, such as his poor health and various emergencies which happen in life, including those where he intentionally slows trading activities for a while for sound business reasons. No, here I'm referring to the situation where the tradesman leaves the business completely and permanently. This is, of course, a very important matter, which should never be undertaken without sufficient consideration and wise counsel. Such decisions can never be justified merely based on some current impulse or reasonable inconveniences that are part of the business, unless wisdom and sound judgment also support the decision. Earlier in this book, we looked at how such decisions might be justified in the case of sudden wealth or one's passion for a retired life. In certain cases, it may be reasonable to leave a calling. We'll discuss some of those now.

BECAUSE OF A HIGHER AUTHORITY

One may be required by a legitimate higher authority to leave their calling. For example, a wife is justified in leaving some calling for which she was educated if her husband desires her to do so or needs her assistance as a helpmeet in some other way. Some citizens may be called to some form of public duty, with or without their consent. Therefore, for purposes of serving the public good, it may be justified that he take on a new calling, at least temporarily. Similarly, when someone is placed under restraint or confinement, either by a magistrate or as part of a lawsuit, it may be necessary that he be discharged from his former calling, and possibly rendered incapable from following it again. So, there are a few of these rare situations.

SITUATIONS OF PHYSICAL DISABILITY

Our callings may be impacted by situations of total disability in body or mind. Not every disease or disability justifies leaving our stations in life. First, our bodies differ as do our appetites and passions. Some are affected by diseases or disabilities in different ways. Therefore, depending on the person, the calling, and other details, one might be justified whereas another might not. For example, the older tradesman, like the pilot of a ship, may still be of great value as an adviser or manager when he becomes unable to do those tasks that require much strength or effort. Such a disability releases the tradesman from his calling only when it renders him no longer able to follow the ends of the calling. When both his body and his employment situation are suffering at the same time, and there's no prospect that he'll be restored to serve the same ends in some capacity, then, by God's providence, he is released from his calling. In such cases, the separation becomes a matter of necessity, not a matter of self-indulgence.

Let the young tradesman consider these things in planning for the future. Let him not be one who spends his income as soon as he receives it but, remaining dependent upon divine providence and being prudent and charitable with what he has, let him remember the days of evil, for they may be many. May he be particularly watchful against extravagance and vice, which can ruin both his physical and his spiritual health and well-being.

Conditions of Mental or Spiritual Weakness

There are certain incapacities of mind that might also discharge someone from their callings. I don't mean that every mental struggle or state of melancholy should excuse us from attending to the proper business of life. One should seek to use the necessary means and apply the appropriate remedies by consulting both the physical physician and the spiritual Physician. It may be there's no better remedy than the application of a little honest diligence in the calling. However, when one's reasoning abilities are utterly clouded or faculties completely weakened that there is no prospect of future recovery, then there is just cause for leaving the calling. Such an affliction is so grievous in its nature and harmful in its effects, that the tradesman should beware of those things that can cause it.

Stay in control of any great passions you might have, whether of love, anger, or fear. Don't be one who provokes God and conscience by violations of truth, justice, and religion. Beware of worldly sorrow. Don't dwell on losses and disappointments. Don't take on more business than you and your circumstances can handle.

Be careful not to abuse what you have. Don't meddle with wild speculations or things that are beyond you. Be humble. Try to maintain a cheerful attitude in all situations. Make the effort to ensure your spiritual well-being, while developing habits that are healthy for your body as well. These things will help you avoid this calamity, which renders many a terror to themselves and to those around them.

BECAUSE OF FINANCIAL DISASTER

Financial problems can make it impossible to carry on one's business. Not every loss or failure of a business or the goods traded will justify leaving our callings. Many have financially been reduced to a very low point but, by the blessing of providence and their own carefulness and hard work, have recovered from financial disasters, and done quite well. However, when business gets to a point where we are unable to maintain goods for sale or trade without going into debt to do so, then it's just and wise that we leave that business. In such cases, a person doesn't really leave his calling, his calling leaves him. Under these circumstances, it's worthwhile for the tradesman to review his behavior to determine if he neglected God in some way, oppressed or acted unjustly toward others, or indulged himself in sinful or extravagant ways. Otherwise, perhaps, it may be that the very sins that have driven him from his business or calling will exclude him from heaven as well.

OUR DAYS ARE NUMBERED

The examples above can be used to help determine when it might be acceptable to resign from a trade, and there may be others. However, the tradesman should always keep it in mind that, even though he may be pursuing his calling with much cheerfulness, diligence and success, one day death will take him from his employment, whatever it might be. "His breath goeth forth, he returneth to his earth; in that very day his thoughts perish." (Psalm 146:4). That day will surely come, if the Lord tarries. And it often comes when it's least expected. Therefore, I advise you to set your soul in order in preparation for that day. It is

OF LEAVING OUR CALLINGS

madness to live in a way in this life that ignores our condition before God, which may in the next day, or next hour, project us into a state of misery and destruction! What senseless stupidity has seized the minds of sinners to think they can stand securely on the edge of such a precipice!

If men weren't so amazingly stupefied by sin, they could never be at ease for a single moment until they were assured of enjoying the one and escaping the other. How do people protect their minds from the terror of knowing they're an enemy of God? How can they open their Bible with any sense of comfort when they read of their own condemnation on every page? One would think that the uncertainty of their own salvation would keep them from sleeping or, at least, cause their sleep to be disturbed by nightmares, not knowing that if they shut their eyes, they may awake in torment. And that the prospect of death and judgment, as near and sure, would fill them with a sense of horror. Indeed, if there were no remedy to the situation, they'd be hopeless. However, the grace and mercy offered by Jesus Christ to repenting and believing sinners is clearly described in the Bible, as are the characters of those who are in a state of salvation or condemnation. So, all that men need to do is to first seriously search the Scriptures and then truthfully examine their own hearts in light of what's written in God's Word to determine which state they're in. Nothing but shear stupidity can cause someone to neglect this matter, or be satisfied with the uncertainty of the awful consequences of death.

Therefore, never rest until you've made peace with God through Jesus Christ, and your heart is purified from every corrupt affection by His Spirit of grace. Then, death can be faced with peace and embraced with joy.

Let me end by mentioning that the same prospect of death and uncertainty of life should motivate every considerate tradesman to set his house in order. For example, make sure that all your books and accounts are up to date. Otherwise, any poor record keeping could present those you leave behind with some serious problems. After you've computed as best you can the true value of your estate, then you should make out your will. This will also make your death easier on your family. After you've settled on reasonable proportions for your wife and children, and if God has blessed you, consider the needs of your other relatives as well. Don't forget to acknowledge the goodness of divine providence by committing some of your wealth to charitable uses.

If the above is done from a principle of faith and love, I believe it represents the best way to financially bless your posterity. Being prepared in this way, death may be expected but need not be feared. You may then cheerfully leave your calling on earth to receive "...the prize of the high calling of God in Christ Jesus." (Philippians 3:14). To Whom be the glory forever and ever. Amen.

SCRIPTURE REFERENCES FOR CHAPTER 9

"If a man die, shall he live again? all the days of my appointed time will I wait, till my change come." (Job 14:14).

"Whatsoever thy hand findeth to do, do it with thy might; for there is no work, nor device, nor knowledge, nor wisdom, in the grave, whither thou goest." (Ecclesiastes 9:10).

"In those days was Hezekiah sick unto death. And Isaiah the prophet the son of Amoz came unto him, and said unto him, Thus saith the LORD, Set thine house in order: for thou shalt die, and not live." (Isaiah 38:1).

"I have fought a good fight, I have finished my course, I have kept the faith: Henceforth there is laid up for me a crown of righteousness, which the Lord, the righteous judge, shall give me at that day: and not to me only, but unto all them also that love his appearing." (2 Timothy 4:7-8).

Scripture Index

Genesis
2:15 — *15*
4:2 — *20*
43:12 — *92*
47:5-6 — *66*

Exodus
20:9 — *15*
20:15 — *70*
20:15,17 — *92*
20:17 — *70*

Leviticus
19:11 — *109*
19:13 — *71*
19:13,35 — *92*
19:14 — *83*
23:3 — *138*
26:21,28 — *29*

Numbers
5:7 — *87*
5:8 — *89*

Deuteronomy
5:29,33 — *36*
6:5 — *131*
8:18 — *64*

16:20 — *71*
25:13-15 — *78*
25:13,16 — *92*
30:11,20 — *148*

Joshua
24:14,16 — *36*

1 Samuel
2:30 — *148*
12:24-25 — *148*

1 Kings
3:6 — *148*
11:28 — *66*

1 Chronicles
28:9 — *37*

2 Chronicles
20:12 — *28*

Ezra
8:21,23 — *28*

Nehemiah
5:13 — *87*
13:31 — *141*

Job
1:20-21 — *125*
1:21 — *111*
2:10 — *125*
5:8 — *23, 28*
14:14 — *151, 156*
20:15,19-20,22,27 — *92*
28:28 — *147*
31:13-14 — *83*

Psalms
9:10 — *119*
9:17 — *98*
14:4 — *135*
15 — *69*
15:1,4 — *109*
15:2 — *96*
15:4 — *101*
26:6 — *137*
34:12-13 — *109*
34:12,14 — *36*
37:7-9,16 — *125*
37:30-31 — *138*
42:11 — *141*
49:16 — *117*
50:18 — *76*
50:19-22 — *109*

56:13—129
62:10—118
63:11—108
66:18—35
78:18-22—125
101:7—109
104:22-23—20
104:23—13, 60
112:3—85
112:5—57
112:7—134
119:2,4,14,115,155, 166—149
119:7—129
119:94—141
119:163—109
127:2—64
146:4—154

Proverbs
1:4—56
1:10, 15—36
2:6—56
3:1-4—36
3:5,7—29
4:7-9,13-15,26—36
4:14-15—53
5:1-2—57
6:1-5—52
6:10-11—67
6:16-17—109
6:21-23—134
8:12, 20-21—57
10:2—29
10:2,6—93
10:4-5—67
10:13—57
10:19—105
11:14—29
11:29—57
12:2,7—93
12:11, 24, 27—67

12:15—56
12:19—95
12:19,22—109
12:27—20
12:28—149
13:5—109
13:11—29
13:13—149
13:16—57
13:20—32, 43
13:22—85
14:1,8,15—57
14:8—41
14:23—20
15:16—126
16:8—93
16:9—29
18:9—67
19:5,9—110
20:4,13—67
20:7—69
20:7,17,21—93
21:6—103
21:15—93
21:17—20, 67
21:20—58
22:8—29
22:29—67
24:3-4—58
24:28—110
24:30-32—55
24:30,34—67
26:12—105
27:8—120
28:8,20—93
28:20—72
30:7-9—126
31:10,13,15,19,27—20

Ecclesiastes
3:1—41, 61

5:3—105
5:10—118
5:12—64
6:9,11—126
9:10—59, 67, 156
10:18—20

Isaiah
3:15—74
8:19—135
26:3—134
38:1—156
45:7,9—126
56:1—71
58:13—137

Jeremiah
9:3,9—110
10:23—29
17:11—93
22:13—29, 93

Ezekiel
16:49—21
22:12,14—94
28:18—94

Daniel
4:27—90

Micah
6:10-11—78
6:12-13—110

Habakkuk
2:13—107

Zechariah
8:16—110
10:6—100

Malachi
2:2—47

SCRIPTURE INDEX

Matthew
3:10,12 — *149*
6:21 — *140*
6:25-26 — *119*
7:12 — *69*
7:21 — *149*
10:16 — *58*
16:26 — *27*
22:21 — *80*

Mark
8:34 — *129*
8:34,38 — *146*

Luke
6:31 — *70*
12:15,24 — *126*
16:11 — *71*
19:8 — *88*

John
6:12 — *61*
6:28-29 — *149*
8:44 — *110*

Acts
5 — *99*
9:36,39 — *21*
20:34-35 — *21*
24:16 — *149*

Romans
1:18, 29, 31 — *94*
6:21-23 — *149*
8:5-8,13 — *143*
8:6 — *129*
8:7 — *130*

1 Corinthians
6:9 — *57, 71*
6:19 — *132*
6:20 — *132*

7:24 — *135*
12:21 — *14*

2 Corinthians
1:12 — *37*

Galatians
6:15 — *130*

Ephesians
2:10 — *130*
4:23 — *130*
4:24-25 — *110*
4:28 — *29, 85*
5:5 — *143*
5:21 — *129*
6:6-7 — *31*

Philippians
3:14 — *156*
4:11 — *126*

Colossians
3:9 — *110*

1 Thessalonians
4:3,7 — *150*
4:6 — *75, 94*

2 Thessalonians
3:5 — *129*
3:12 — *15*

1 Timothy
5:8 — *16*
5:13 — *21*
6:6,11 — *126*

2 Timothy
2:22 — *37*
4:7-8 — *156*

Titus
2:6 — *37*
2:12 — *39, 64, 71, 145*
2:13-14 — *150*
3:14 — *21, 29*

Hebrews
4:13 — *132*
5:8-9 — *150*
12:14-15 — *150*
12:28-29 — *131*
13:5 — *120*
11:1 — *135*

James
1:5 — *56*

1st Peter
1:23 — *130*
4:14-15 — *54*

2nd Peter
1:2 — *129*
3:10-11 — *150*

Revelation
22:15 — *110*

Homeschool Record Keeping Just Got Easier...

Homeschool P.R.O. is a new software program recently developed by Vision Harvest, a new home-based business that is operated by a homeschooling family. The program reduces the time homeschooling parents spend Planning, Recording, and Organizing their homeschool. They can create schedules for students using Homeschool P.R.O.'s built-in scheduling system. From the data entered into this schedule, grades can easily be calculated and averaged; lessons can be managed and printed. There's even an attendance calendar to keep track of attendance, absences, etc. Create journals to jot down notes, reading lists, chores, etc. And much more.

Try Homeschool P.R.O. for yourself by downloading the trial license copy (of the full version) free of charge from our website. You will be pleased with its price too.

- *Fast*
- *Friendly*
- *Affordable*

Vision Harvest, Inc.
P.O. Box 680, Haymarket, VA 20168
703-754-0696 • info@vision-harvest.com

www.vision-harvest.com/hspro